Herta F. Kraupa-T

Boxers

Management, Care, Feeding, Sickness, Breeding
With a Special Chapter on Understanding Boxers

Translated from the German by Elizabeth D. Crawford

With color photographs by well-known animal photographers
and drawings by György Jankovics

American Advisory Editor: Matthew M. Vriends, Ph D

BARRON'S

All inquiries should be addressed to:
Barron's Educational Series, Inc.
250 Wireless Boulevard
Hauppauge, NY 11788

Library of Congress Catalog Card No. 88-3335

International Standard Book No. 0-8120-4036-8

Library of Congress Cataloging-in-Publication Data

Kraupa-Tuskany, Herta F.
   Boxers: everything about purchase, care, feeding,
breeding, and training.

   Translation of: Boxer.
   Includes index.
   1. Boxers (Dogs) I. Title
SF429.B75K7313   1988   636.7'3   88-3335
ISBN 0-8120-4036-8

PRINTED IN CHINA

456   9770   11 10 9 8

The photographs on the covers show:
Front cover: Boxer bitch Polly with her puppy.
Inside front cover: Pedigreed young male boxer.
Inside back cover: The four-year-old male Korbinian
von Donnersburg.
Back cover: Above: A boxer running; below: two male
boxers.

The AKC Boxer Standard is reprinted with the permission of The American Kennel Club.

Herta F. Kraupa-Tuskany,
with many years' experience in keeping and breeding
boxers, is the author of successful animal books,
among them *Ponies: A Complete Pet Owners Manual*

Advice and Warning
   This book is concerned with buying, keeping, and
raising boxers. The publisher and the author think it is
important to point out that the advice and information
for boxer maintenance applies to healthy, normally developed animals. Anyone who buys an adult boxer or
acquires one from an animal shelter must consider that
the animal may have behavioral problems and may, for
example, bite without apparent provocation (see page
55). Such anxiety biters are dangerous to the owner as
well as to the general public.
   Caution is further advised in the association of children with a boxer (see page 26), in meetings with other
dogs (see page 52), in exercising the dog without a
lead (see pages 24 and 39), and in walking a leashed
boxer in winter on snow and ice (see page 30).
   Even well-trained and carefully supervised dogs may
occasionally harm other people's property or even
cause accidents. Adequate insurance protection is in
your own best interest; dog liability insurance is
strongly recommended.

Contents

Contents

Preface

My first boxer was given to me by friends. They knew that I was looking for a good watchdog for our house and that my family at one time kept French bulldogs. Since these original "bullies," which, like the boxer, belong to the hounds, are not suitable watchdogs, however, my friends surprised me with a boxer puppy. It was an especially beautiful little dog, Bonita, that won my heart from the first moment. For more than 30 years boxers have been the true friends, companions, and protectors of me and my family. Thus I have become very familiar with the character of the boxer and I know how to value its qualities: its devotion and great intelligence, its originality, its energy, its even disposition, and its love of children — not to mention its good nature, which does not in any way contradict the fact that the boxer is a very reliable watchdog, one to be reckoned with.

I once read that a boxer is a dog for beginners. This gives the impression that no special knowledge is necessary for keeping a boxer. After my years of experience with boxers, I cannot share this view, for an owner who knows nothing of this breed can expose his or her boxer to various dangers, and the dog itself can cause much mischief for which the owner is then responsible. Basic knowledge of the nature of the boxer and of the proper care and training are prerequisites for the well-being of the dog and a good life with it. In this book I wish to share the experience I have gathered in dealing with boxers. It should be a comprehensive source of advice to all who are keeping a boxer for the first time, but it should also convey new suggestions and information to experienced boxer keepers.

In a brief portrait of the boxer I explain the origins of the breed and introduce the boxer along with the basic rules of the standard. At this point the much debated question of ear cropping is addressed.

Next I go into some detail about what you should consider when buying a boxer — even if it is not the first — so that you can avoid making a wrong choice.

The essentials of taking care of puppies and of the proper care and control of the grown boxer are found in the chapter entitled Maintenance and Care, which closes with detailed explanations of proper feeding.

The importance of boxer training, which should begin in puppyhood, is discussed in the chapter on training. Anyone who would like to have boxer puppies will find important and useful advice in the chapter on breeding and raising puppies.

A special chapter considers the character and behavior patterns of the boxer, for understanding them is the key to a good life together. The more lovingly, understandingly, yet at the same time consistently you treat your boxer, the more pleasure you will have in this good-natured, understanding, and loyal comrade.

Herta F. Kraupa-Tuskany

Author and publisher thank all who have worked together on this book: the photographers for the extraordinarily beautiful photographs, the artist György Jankovics for his informative drawings, and the veterinarian Dr. Gabriele Wiesner for the expert advice on the chapter Health Maintenance and Sickness.

A Brief Portrait of the Boxer

How the Breed Began

The boxer originated in Asia. Its developmental history begins in antiquity with the Tibetan wolf. This was the ancestor of the Tibetan dog, from which all the hounds are descended. These are differentiated from other dog breeds by a powerful head with a broad muzzle and a strong set of teeth as well as by their strong body build. Over an immense period of time, Tibetan dogs spread from Asia across Europe.

The Molossian Hound
In Greece, long before our time, the famous tribe of the Molossians made use of these brave, hardy animals as fighting and herding hounds and gave their name to them. Molossian hounds continued to be much desired until after the fall of Rome and into the Middle Ages. At the same time the Celts and the Germanic tribes in Northern Europe had bred mastiff dog breeds; these were especially successful in Britain. Drawing a definite distinction between the breeds of that day — Molossian and the British mastiff, or bulldog — is scarcely possible today. For centuries they were both indispensable helpers to the tribes and peoples of Europe in war and in hunting.

The Bullenbeisser
Bullenbeissers (bull biters) were used above all for tracking and attacking bears, wolves, and the powerful aurochs (a wild ox). They were bred into two types according to their usefulness in the hunt: a heavy one, the large or Danzig bulldog, and a lighter or Brabant bulldog (the names indicate the places where they were bred successfully). With the small, brave bulldog began the traceable history of the boxer, which is a German breed. The small bulldog must possess strength, bravery, endurance, and skill, but also speed to preserve itself in the hunt for wild boar and stags and in the pursuit of bulls and large herds of cattle. These outstanding characteristics persist in their descendants to the present day.

From Bullenbeisser to Boxer
When hunting changed fundamentally with the invention of firearms and when cattle were bred within the country itself, rather than being driven from other lands, there was no more work for the bulldog. Only as a faithful watchdog, as a house dog, did it continue to serve human beings. The dog was now known popularly as the boxer. Uncontrolled breeding resulted in various types; the breed was neglected. At the end of the last century a few boxer enthusiasts joined together and with energy and idealism took charge of the regulation and improvement of the breed. They founded a boxer club in Munich in 1895. There was a show the following year, and since 1904 an internationally recognized studbook has been maintained. The standard that was established one year later has, except for a trifling change in the size measurement, remained in force to this day.

The first boxer was brought to the United States from Switzerland in 1903. The American Kennel Club (AKC) registered the first boxer born in the United States of America in 1904. In the early 1940s the boxer began to achieve widespread acceptance here.

How the Boxer Looks — The AKC Boxer Standard

A standard is a definition of all breed characteristics for an ideal example of the dog in question. It stands as a firm guiding principle for all breeders and for the judging at shows, the so-called specialty shows. The standard can be obtained from the American Boxer Club (see page 43). Breed characteristics include qualities of temperament and character as well as the external features. Besides his qualifications as a family dog the boxer must also have those of a watchdog, companion, and working dog: courage, fixity of purpose, loyalty, hardiness, and energy, as well as an extraordinary urge to protect. Its intelligence and ability and eagerness to learn suit the boxer for many different duties.

General Appearance

The boxer is a medium-sized, sturdy dog, of square build, with short back, strong limbs, and short, tight-fitting coat. The musculature, well developed, should be clean and hard and appear smooth (not bulging) under taut skin. Movements should denote energy. The gait is firm yet elastic (springy), the stride free and ground covering, the carriage proud and noble. Developed to serve the multiple purposes of guard, working, and escort dog, it must combine elegance with substance and ample power, not alone for beauty but to ensure the speed, dexterity, and jumping ability essential to arduous hiking, riding expedition, police or military duty. Only a body whose individual parts are built to withstand the most strenuous efforts, assembled as a complete and harmonious whole, can respond to these combined demands. Therefore, to be at its highest efficiency it must never be plump or heavy and although equipped for great speed, it must never be racy.

The head imparts to the boxer a unique stamp, peculiar to it alone. It must be in perfect proportion to the body, never small in comparison to the overall picture. The muzzle is its most distinctive feature, and great value is placed on its being of correct form and in absolute proper proportion to the skull.

In judging the boxer, first consideration should be given to general appearance; next, overall balance, including the desired proportions of the individual parts of the body to each other, as well as the relation of substance to elegance — to which an attractive color or arresting style may contribute. Special attention is devoted to the head, after which the dog's individual components are examined for their correct construction and function, and efficiency of gait evaluated.

General Faults: Head not typical, plump, bulldog appearance, light bone, lack of balance, bad condition, lack of noble bearing.

Head

The beauty of the head depends upon the harmonious proportion of the muzzle to the skull. The muzzle should always appear powerful, never in its relationship to the skull. The head should be clean, not showing deep wrinkles. Folds normally appear upon the forehead when the ears are erect, and they are always indicated from the lower edge of the stop running downward on both sides of the muzzle. The dark mask is confined to the muzzle and is in distinct contrast to the color of the head. Any extension of the mask to the skull, other than dark shading around the eyes, creates a somber, undesirable expression. When white replaces any of the black mask, the path of any upward extension should be between the eyes. The muzzle is powerfully developed in length, width, and depth. It is not pointed, narrow, short, or shallow. Its shape is influenced first through the formation of both jawbones, second through the placement of the teeth, and third through the texture of the lips.

The boxer is normally undershot. Therefore, the lower jaw protrudes beyond the upper and curves slightly upward. The upper jaw is broad where attached to the skull and maintains this breadth except for a very slight tapering to the front. The incisor teeth of the lower jaw are in a straight line, the canines preferably up front in the same line to give the jaw the greatest possible width. The line of incisors in the upper jaw is slightly convex toward the front. The upper corner incisors should fit snugly in back of the lower canine teeth on each side, reflecting the symmetry essential to the creation of a sound, non-slip bite.

The lips, which complete the formation of the muzzle, should meet evenly. The upper lip is thick and padded, filling out the frontal space created by the projection of the lower jaw. It rests

A Brief Portrait of the Boxer

on the edge of the lower lip and, laterally, is supported by the fangs (canines) of the lower jaw. Therefore, these fangs must stand far apart and be long enough that the front surface of the muzzle is broad and squarish and, when viewed from the side, forms an obtuse angle with the topline of the muzzle. Overprotrusion of the overlip or underlip is undesirable. The chin should be perceptible when viewed from the sides as well as from the front without being overrepandous (rising above the bite line) as in the bulldog. The boxer must not show teeth or tongue when the mouth is closed. Excessive flews are not desirable.

The top of the skull is slightly arched, not rotund, flat, noticeably broad, and the occiput not too pronounced. The forehead forms a distinct stop with the topline of the muzzle, which must not be forced like that of a bulldog. It should not slant down (down-faced), nor should it be dished, although the tip of the nose should lie somewhat higher than the root of the muzzle. The forehead shows just a slight furrow between the eyes. The cheeks, although covering powerful masseter muscles compatible with the strong set of teeth, should be relatively flat and not bulge, maintaining the clean lines of the skull. They taper into the muzzle in a slight, graceful curve. The ears are set at the highest points of the sides of the skull, cut rather long without too broad a shell, and are carried erect. The dark brown eyes, not too small, protruding, or deep set, are encircled by dark hair and should impart an alert, intelligent expression. Their mood-mirroring quality combined with the mobile skin furrowing of the forehead gives the boxer head its unique degree of expressiveness. The nose is broad and black, very slightly turned up; the nostrils broad, with the nasolabial line running between them down through the upper lip, which, however, must not be split.

Faults: Lack of nobility and expression, somber face, unserviceable bite. Pinscher or bulldog head, sloping topline of muzzle, muzzle too light for skull, too pointed a bite (snipy). Teeth or tongue showing with mouth closed, driveling, split upper lip. Poor ear carriage, light ("bird of prey") eyes.

Neck

Round, of ample length, not too short; strong, muscular, and clean throughout, without dewlap; distinctly marked nape with an elegant arch running down to the back.
Fault: Dewlap.

Body

In profile, the build is of square proportions in that a horizontal line from the front of the forechest to the rear projection of the upper thigh should equal a vertical line dropped from the top of the withers to the ground.

Chest and Forequarters

The brisket is deep, reaching down to the elbows; the depth of the body at the lowest point of the brisket equals half the height of the dog at the withers. The ribs, extending far to the rear, are well arched but not barrel shaped. Chest of fair width and forechest well defined, being easily visible from the side. The loins are short and muscular; the lower stomach line, lightly tucked up, blends into a graceful curve to the rear. The shoulders are long and sloping, close lying and not excessively covered with muscle. The upper arm is long, closely approaching a right angle to the shoulder blade. The forelegs, viewed from the front, are straight, stand parallel to each other, and have strong, firmly joined bones. The elbows should not press too closely to the chest wall or stand off visibly from it. The forearm is straight, long, and firmly muscled. The pastern joint is clearly defined but not distended. The pastern is strong and distinct, slightly slanting, but standing almost perpendicular to the ground.

A Brief Portrait of the Boxer

The dewclaws may be removed as a safety precaution. Feet should be compact, turning neither in nor out, with tightly arched toes (cat feet) and tough pads.

Faults: Chest too broad, too shallow, or too deep in front; loose or overmuscled shoulders; chest hanging between shoulders; tied-in or bowed-out elbows; turned feet; hare feet; hollow flanks; hanging stomach.

Back

The withers should be clearly defined as the highest point of the back; the whole back short, straight, and muscular with a firm topline.

Faults: Roach back, sway back, thin lean back, long narrow loins, weak union with croup.

Hindquarters

Strongly muscled with angulation in balance with that of forequarters. The thighs broad and curved, the breech musculature hard and strongly developed. Croup slightly sloped, flat, and broad. Tail attachment high rather than low. Tail clipped, carried upward. Pelvis long and, in females especially, broad. Upper and lower thigh long, leg well angulated with a clearly defined, well-let-down hock joint. In standing position, the leg below the hock joint (metatarsus) should be practically perpendicular to the ground, with a slight rearward slope permissible. Viewed from behind, the hind legs should be straight, with the hock joints leaning neither in nor out. The metatarsus should be short, clean, and strong, supported by powerful rear pads. The rear toes just a little longer than the front toes, but similar in all other respects. Dewclaws, if any, may be removed.

Faults: Too rounded, too narrow, or falling off of croup; low-set tail; higher in back than in front; steep, stiff, or too slightly angulated hindquarters; light thighs; bowed or crooked legs; cow hocks; overangulated hock joints (sickle hocks); long metatarsus (high hocks); hare feet; hindquarters too far under or too far behind.

Gait

Viewed from the side, proper front and rear angulation is manifested in a smoothly efficient, level-backed, ground-covering stride with powerful drive emanating from a freely operating rear. Although the front legs do not contribute impelling power, adequate "reach" should be evident to prevent interference, overlap or "side winding" (crabbing). Viewed from the front, the shoulders should remain trim and the elbows not flare out. The legs are parallel until gaiting narrows the track in proportion to increasing speed, then the legs come in under the body but should never cross. The line from the shoulder down through the legs should remain straight, although not necessarily perpendicular to the ground. Viewed from the rear, a boxer's breech should not roll. The hind feet should "dig in" and track relatively true with the front. Again, as speed increases, the normally broad rear track will become narrower.

Faults: Stilted or inefficient gait, pounding, paddling or flailing out of front legs, rolling or waddling gait, tottering hock joints, crossing over or interference—front or rear, lack of smoothness.

Height

Adult males—22 $\frac{1}{2}$ to 25 inches (57–63.5 cm); females—21 to 23 $\frac{1}{2}$ inches (53–59.7 cm) at the withers. Males should not go under the minimum nor females over the maximum.

Coat

Short, shiny, lying smooth and tight to the body.

Color

The colors are fawn and brindle. Fawn in various shades from light tan to dark deer red or mahogany, the deep colors preferred. The brindle variety should have clearly defined black stripes on fawn background. White markings on fawn or brindle dogs are not to be rejected and are often very attractive but must be limited to one-third of the ground color and are not desirable on the back of the torso proper. On the face, white may replace a part or all of the otherwise essential black mask. However, these white markings should be of such distribution as to enhance and not detract from true boxer expression.

Character and Temperament

These are of paramount importance in the boxer. Instinctively a "hearing" guard dog, its bearing is alert, dignified, and self-assured, even at rest. In the show ring, its behavior should exhibit constrained animation. With family and friends, its temperament is fundamentally playful, yet patient and stoical with children. Deliberate and wary with strangers, it will exhibit curiosity, but, most importantly, fearless courage and tenacity if threatened. However, it responds promptly to friendly overtures when honestly rendered. Its intelligence, loyal affection, and tractability to discipline make it a highly desirable companion. **Faults:** Lack of dignity and alertness, shyness, cowardice, treachery, and viciousness (belligerency toward other dogs should not be considered viciousness).

Disqualifications

Boxers with white or black ground color, or entirely white or black, or any color other than fawn or brindle. (White markings, when present, must not exceed one-third of the ground color.)

Cropped Ears?

For some time, animal protectors have promoted a law against cropping. As a result, cropping has been legally forbidden in certain states and in some countries. The puppies are thus spared the uncomfortable high binding or plastering of their ear tips in the first period after the cropping. In the controversy over the practice of ear cropping the question that first arises is, what are the grounds for this centuries-old custom? In battles against other dogs, in the harrying of bulls, and

On the left a boxer with uncropped ears, on the right one with cropped ears. Cropping is not permitted in some countries.

in the hunt, the ancestors of our boxers were exposed to the desperate attempts at defense and the angry attacks of their opponents. The unprotected hanging ears of the dog were especially endangered. Painful and difficult-to-heal wounds of depending ear flaps, which the dog could not lick like wounds on other places on its body, moved the men of those bygone times to carefully shorten the ears of puppies. They took as their example the wolf and the other large wild animals, which all were provided by nature with upstanding ears. The practice of ear cropping has been maintained to the present day as a protection for the sometimes pugnacious boxer. Moreover, since the short, sharp ears are well-suited to its bearing, stature, and demeanor, this form is retained in most of the United States, and many other countries. However, cropping, which may only be done legally by a veterinarian and under full anesthesia, should be understood not as a fashion but as a measure for the dog's well-being. Aside from the danger of wounds, dogs with hanging ears frequently suffer from wearison, painful ear infections (see page 29).

Docked Tails?

The docking of the tail, also a very old practice, continues to be permitted, since the usefulness of this measure to the dog is considered greater than the harm. The little tail of the puppy is shortened in the first two to four days after its birth. It is a seconds-long procedure, which the little boxer scarcely notices; healing proceeds very quickly. Injury by breaking its tail is then no longer possible.

The Boxer as Family and Working Dog

The boxer's qualities are responsible for its development from the purely working dog of bygone days to an ideal family dog, a loyal house companion who will protect the family and its home.

● It is watchful—but not a yelper, not a dog that barks mindlessly or endlessly.
● It is brave, a daredevil—but not malicious or treacherous.
● It allows itself to be trained easily, is obedient— but never subservient.
● It loves to play—but it is not restless or nervous.
● It is loving and needs love—but will not be tiresome.

The boxer is easy to care for, an added argument for its particular suitability as a family dog. The boxer's high capabilities and good temperamental qualities also equip it to be a working dog; that is, it can be trained as a police dog and as a first-aid dog or a companion dog.

What to Consider Before You Buy

Before You Decide to Get a Boxer

There are various important questions you need to weigh so that you don't run into unforeseen problems and so that the dog finds a good home where it can remain all its life. For a dog, the change from one master to another or being sent to an animal shelter is the worst thing that could happen. The boxer feels entirely bound to its master and to the family it lives with. Every interruption of this bond is painful. Therefore, when you get a dog, you take on the entire responsibility for this living being—indeed, for many years to come.

Your boxer is attached to you alone, and complete acceptance of your behavior—whatever it is—is a part of its nature. A normal dog does not protect itself against bad or unfair treatment, even if it were in a position to do so. Therefore you should repay its trust, loyalty, and devotion to you with love, understanding, and the proper care and training.

Accommodations: The boxer is basically a quiet dog. In a house or an apartment it keeps quite still (except for the first year of life). It needs much exercise, however, a great deal of movement. Therefore a boxer is not suited for life in a small apartment. A house with a yard is ideal. You can keep a boxer in a larger apartment if your neighborhood has green areas where you can walk it. In any case, however, it's essential that you go on excursions and hikes with it or work with it regularly in a training area. Living outdoors exclusively, in a run or in a yard with a doghouse, is not suitable for a boxer.

Legal Considerations for the Dog Owner: If you keep a dog you must observe some administrative and legal rules.

Tenants: If you are a renter in an apartment or a house you need a written agreement (in the lease) from your landlord for keeping a dog. The landlord may only retract this permission in certain very specific exceptional cases.

Animal protection: Important duties are imposed on the dog owner. Your boxer should
- be properly housed
- receive adequate, appropriate feeding and care
- get sufficient exercise
- not be kept on a chain
- not be allowed to run loose

Dog license: In most areas buying a dog license is also one of the duties of the dog owner. You must report your dog—puppies, too—to the local authorities within 10 days after you get it.

Keeping the sidewalks clean: You must be careful that your dog does not foul the sidewalk during its walk. In some areas "pooper-scooper" laws may impose a heavy fine on those who do not clean up after their pets.

Dog Liability Insurance: Every boxer is likely to get into trouble at least once in its life—in a fight with other dogs, for example, or through property damage—and therefore dog liability insurance is strongly advised.

Time Expenditure: Very often the time and attention that your boxer needs is underestimated. You cannot limit your attention without injury to the animal, however. Therefore you should leave the puppy or the young dog alone only for short periods of time and should play with it a great deal in order to have undivided pleasure with your boxer later. Even the grown dog needs regular attention and a great deal of exercise. This, besides the care and the feeding, demand a not insubstantial portion of your daily time. Of course you can leave a well-behaved boxer alone for a few hours now and again, but only in exceptional cases should you leave it for a whole day. Otherwise it suffers a great deal; it will never get used to a long period of being alone but becomes deadened or breaks something in protest and begins to misbehave. Families whose members are busy all day long should forego getting a boxer.

Important: Another problem that you must consider before getting a boxer is the care of your dog during your absence (see page 28) and on trips (see page 27).

The Cost of Keeping a Boxer: You should bear in mind in all the expenditures for your boxer that false economy can affect the health and the well-being of the dog.

Buying: Boxers from the kennel of a recognized breeder command quite a high price. This is in line with their character, their interior and external quality, the fact that they approach the standard. A boxer with proper papers can cost well over $500; a boxer without a pedigree is, on the other hand, much more economical.

Equipment: It doesn't pay to skimp on the equipment, for it should not only be functional but also solid and sturdy. Besides, these expenditures average out over a long time. The first things to be bought are the not very costly puppy equipment, of which a big sleeping basket with mattress and cover is the most expensive.

Maintenance: The cost of maintenance is chiefly in the feeding cost. Depending on the kind of feed and the amount your dog eats you must figure on $65 or more per month.

Dog license and insurance: The cost of a license varies, depending on where you live; in large cities it is usually higher than in rural areas. Also different are the premiums for dog health insurance and for dog liability insurance.

Other costs: Costs of worming occur regularly; also, for the nonimmunized dog there will be the expense of inoculations and veterinary treatment. In addition, sometimes there is the application fee for membership in a boxer club or society.

Puppy or Adult Dog?

The puppy: If particular circumstances don't force you to choose a grown dog, I would advise you to get a puppy. There are a number of reasons for this. Not only will you have great delight in the lively little fellow, but its bonding to you will develop from the beginning as you

The puppies' ability and character are already recognizable in their play.

train and care for it; furthermore, during the first months of its young life, its attachment to one family member becomes absolutely firm. During this period of imprinting you can mold its character, encourage its good qualities, and provide it with the right training that is so important for your life together.

The adult boxer: If you want to take an already grown boxer—perhaps from an animal shelter to ease its lot or because you want a watchdog for your home right away— find out as much as you can beforehand about the animal's earlier circumstances. If you have much love, patience, and understanding for the breed a grown boxer can in principle also be good to have and may even be trainable to some extent. Characteristics that are firmly anchored in its temperament, long-practiced habits, or bad behavior are, however, unlikely to be influenced, especially in an older animal.

Female or Male Dog?

Whether you decide on a male or a female is an important but difficult question. There are many arguments for and against both sexes. Of course there are generalizations: The female is more dependent and dependable than the male; the male is supposed to have more strength and be braver, but also to have the urge to fight and roam. From the experience I have gained in decades of dealing with boxer males and females, I cannot verify these generalizations. The behavior of any boxer, no matter which sex, depends primarily on its own gifts, nature, and character. Secondarily its behavior may in large measure be influenced by treatment, rearing, and, if necessary, also by the training it undergoes.

A female: is in heat twice a year (see page 62). In connection with this there are some inconveniences, such as supervision of the animal and dealing with the discharge. Keeping a female demands an especially strong sense of responsibility if you want to guard against her having undesirable puppies. Prevention by means of medication or sterilization is possible, but I personally feel this is an avoidable interference in the natural course of the animal's life.

A male: is usually always eager to mate. This means that as soon as your dog gets the scent of a female in heat or if he finds a favorite in the neighborhood who attracts him irresistibly, you must supervise him just as closely as a female in heat. Otherwise you must reckon that he will persistently try to make his way to the "object of his desires" with all kinds of tricks and that he will stay away for long periods and will be exposed to many dangers, especially to that of traffic. You should further consider that a male is harder to lead than a female because of his size and strength. This is especially important if the dog is going to be lead by older people or by children.

One Dog or Two Companions?

A single dog: is the easiest to have in a family. It bonds quickly and completely to the human and considers him or her its companion. It feels entirely content in its attachment to the family and as "sole ruler." Even among boxers there are so-called loners.

Fetching. When the boxer has fetched the stick it must hold it in its mouth and remain in the "sit" position until it receives the command "out"; then the puppy lays the stick in the hand of its master.

Two companions: Most boxers are sociable, and the companionship, the constant scuffling, and the play with their comrades are necessary for their development and increasing their body strength. A house with the largest possible yard is an absolute requirement if you are to be able to enjoy having two or more boxers. For very large or rather isolated establishments two boxers as watchdogs are a splendid protection.

A pair is a natural ideal. But if you don't intend to breed, keeping them is difficult unless the female is spayed.

Two males can get along with each other if they have grown up together or if a puppy is paired with an adult dog. Unfortunately, however, even in these cases incompatibility sometimes occurs. It is usually difficult if two already grown males are expected to get used to one another.

Keeping two females is seldom attempted, for recurring quarrels can develop between them, even with females that have grown up together.

Caution: Walking two such strong dogs on the lead—at least until they can "heel"—demands a great deal of strength and can be really dangerous in winter in slush or ice.

Buying Advice

The Right Time to Buy

In many cases the time to buy depends on personal factors, but if you can freely determine the time, I advise you to buy in early summer. The summer and fall months are more suitable in many respects for raising a puppy than are the cold seasons, with rain, snow, and ice. Ordinarily, bitches whelp in spring and late fall. The puppies remain with the mother for about 8 to 12 weeks, so they are usually available in the beginning of summer or in the winter.

Where You Can Get a Boxer

From the Breeder: Of all the many possibilities, the best is to buy from a recognized boxer breeder. To avoid a buying mistake that can have sad consequences for you and for the dog, you had best turn to the American Boxer Club (address, see page 67). From them you will receive a list of the recognized breeders and learn which is able to sell you a puppy or a suitable dog at this time. The breeder will give you reliable advice. The puppies will conform to the standard and are immunized and wormed. Furthermore, as well as the certified pedigree you will receive a feeding plan for the first few days and the inoculation data. If you can, compare several breeders before you buy. In some kennels there is a greater choice of puppies of different ages; they are housed in pens. In smaller establishments the choice is narrower, to be sure, but the individual puppies usually have had especially loving individual care and attention. This is very beneficial to their whole development.

From the Pet Shop: If you go through a pet store to get a boxer from a recognized breeder, you must forego the pleasure of choosing your boxer for yourself. In this case, however, you can count on getting a healthy boxer puppy with a certified pedigree. I must warn you against buying from any pet shop in which the puppies of various breeds are kept in narrow cages or showcases. It happens over and over again that such puppies have been infected, that they are intimidated—that is, they have suffered emotional and bodily harm—and that their origins cannot be documented or that the pedigrees are not valid.

From a Private Breeder: In the classified section of many newspapers and magazines there is a heading Pets for Sale. Here you will find the ads of the owners of bitches who "should have puppies once in her life" (a subject that is discussed more on page 62). The price of such puppies is usually far less than that of a puppy from a recognized kennel, especially if they have no papers. It is uncertain whether they are purebred. Buying such puppies is therefore a matter of trust to an exceptional degree. You can have luck and encounter a responsible private breeder who has kept the dog well, bred her with a good boxer male, and raised the puppies with understanding and love. These young boxers have spent their first days in close contact with a family, they grow up in house and yard, and develop free and healthy. Unfortunately, however, there are also "hobby breeders" who allow their females to breed only for the profit involved and skimp on raising the puppies, which they often remove from the mother too early.

From an Animal Shelter: If you want to get your boxer from an animal shelter you will certainly be doing the animal a good turn. Before doing so, however, find out about its behavior and its earlier existence, so far as it is known. With dogs that have been given to an animal shelter there is always the possibility of emotional damage or a behavioral disturbance. Such dogs, who of course also need a home and help, should only be in the hands of a very experienced and patient person.

Where You Should Not Buy Your Boxer: There are many dog dealers that do not maintain a connection with a related large kennel and continuously offer dogs of various breeds obtained from the so-called "puppy mills." These are concerned only with profit. If you don't want to run the danger of getting a weak, sick, or even behaviorally disturbed dog, you should not get your dog from such a large dealer. Under no circumstances should you "order" your boxer from a mail-order business. Doing so sustains a business practice by which the animals are made to suffer very much and the buyer takes an enormous risk.

What to Look for When Buying

The Age of the Puppy
The best time to take a puppy away from its mother and littermates to its new home is the time between the eighth and the twelfth week of life. Don't let yourself be persuaded to buy a younger puppy, for it is not yet weaned. It needs the warmth of the nest as well as the companionship and the conflicts with its brothers and sisters. If, on the other hand, the puppy has been with its mother somewhat longer than 12 weeks, you can easily take it. The only drawback is that you will be a little late in beginning to get it to feel at home and getting started with training.

Lifting the puppy: One hand grasps the chest, the other supports the rear end.

Health Status
Notice first whether the dogs are kept well and their kennel is clean. This is a prerequisite for their health and well-being.

The important signs of a healthy puppy are:
- Smooth, shining fur, clear eyes, straight back, and straight legs.
- The "toe walking" due to the tightly arched toes that is typical of the boxer is already recognizable in the puppy, despite its fat, clumsy feet.
- A healthy puppy is lively, alert, and curious. It may be defeated but may not be scared or too timid.

Thinness, dull fur, and teary eyes are signs of sickness or bad maintenance of the puppies. If you have any doubts, ask a boxer fancier or a veterinarian who specializes in dogs to look at the puppies and to judge. If it is at all possible, see the parent animals too. This way you will get an approximate idea of the later size and appearance of your boxer.

Immunization, Worming, and Feeding Plan
The basic immunizations can be done at the seventh week. Therefore the puppy bought from any responsible breeder or from a reliable pet store will already have been inoculated and will come to its new owner with the necessary immunization papers. All further inoculations that your boxer must have during its lifetime (see page 58) will be entered in these papers. Find out before you get your puppy if it has been wormed. Early worming is especially important for the development of the young boxer. Most breeders give the buyer very precise instructions for the puppy's

Boxer puppies at play. Through curious exploration the puppies gain information about their environment and learn the right behavior.

Buying Advice

further feeding. Should this not be the case, ask how it has been fed up to now and ask for a written feeding plan. A sudden change to other quantities and kinds of food often produces stomach and intestinal upsets.

The carriage of a healthy, powerful boxer male.

Pedigree Papers

If you plan to breed your boxer or to show it or if it is going to take part in trials, a registered pedigree is essential. "Registered" means that the dog is listed in the records of the American Kennel Club, and often of the appropriate boxer club, which contain the breed lines of its ancestors as well those of all boxers, for many decades, back to the beginning of the boxer breed. This studbook is recognized internationally by the Fédération Cynologique Internationale (FCI). Check out the pedigree by means of an inquiry to a dog show exhibitor, for there are also proofs of bloodlines that are unsuitable for your purposes. You can do without pedigree papers for a family dog whose only duty will be to be your true friend and watchdog.

The boxer and children. Complete trust exists between five-week-old puppy Assi and three-year-old Amadeo.

Maintenance and Care

Bringing Home Your New Pet

Morning is the best time to collect your new boxer. Then the new puppy has enough time to sniff around the strange environment and to get somewhat accustomed to its new home.

The Right Way to Pick a Puppy Up: If you haven't yet had experience with a lively little puppy, before you leave have the breeder show you the right way to pick one up: Hold it around the chest with one hand and support its rear end with the other (see drawing page 16).

It's wrong:
● to bend the little legs to one side, for the bones of puppies are still not firm
● to lift or drag the puppy by the front legs
● to grasp the puppy by the skin at the back of the neck, as used to be done commonly

Important: Hold your little boxer securely if you carry it on your arm or take it in your lap in the car. With a sudden movement it can very easily fall down.

The Trip Home: If you have taken an adult boxer, find out if you can before you bring it home how it tolerates riding in a car. Otherwise ask the owner to give the dog an appropriate medication or get it yourself from the veterinarian. In the car the dog will be placed in the backseat—never in front. Have a family member sit beside it, hold it, stroke it, and talk to it; this will reassure it in the new situation. Put a collar on it before the start of the journey, and attach a short lead so that you have it under control. Since dogs are very sensitive to moving air, the car windows must remain closed. A puppy will feel best in a little basket or on a large cushion that you hold on your lap. It needs security at this point. Have a paper towel or a newspaper ready for emergencies. Most puppies survive the first journey very well.

Getting Used to Unfamiliar Surroundings

Everything is new, everything is strange to the boxer when it comes into your home. The familiar smell of its mother, brothers, and sisters, their nearness and warmth, are missing.

The First Hours: At first curiosity is stronger than the feeling of strangeness. The puppy runs excitedly around and sniffs everything: it explores its new surroundings with its nose. It is best if you leave it alone for these first few minutes. Keep an old newspaper handy, however, and if it begins to increase its sniffing and makes preparations to squat, set it on the newspaper so that it can relieve itself, that is, can urinate or have a bowel movement. This is the first step in housebreaking. If it makes a puddle on your rug, please don't punish it. The punishment will be unsuccessful, because it won't understand, but it can very easily become anxious. The chapter on training (see page 37) explains how to patiently housebreak the puppy.

The First Days: Always remember that the way you treat your puppy in the first days and weeks, how you reassure it and train it, is of great importance for its development and later behavior. In the acclimation period it needs much love and care. Right away, show it the feeding dish, water dish, and sleeping place, which will give it security. Do not leave the puppy alone at all for the first few days. Feelings of loneliness cause many a puppy to develop bad habits: it chews on its basket, on the rug, or on shoes; it scratches on doors or the carpet; for comfort it lies on an armchair or climbs on a bed, where it feels less lonely. It looks for a living being to whom it can connect. This doesn't mean, however, that you should fuss with it ceaselessly; your presence in itself gives it some security. Confusion, noise, and hectic activity are just as bad for it as too little attention. Therefore it's best to wait a few days before you show the new puppy to your friends and acquaintances, who are sure to be curious about the little dog but will also understand that it needs a quiet time to get accustomed to its new surroundings. It should also not be bewildered by too many people, for at first it must get to know its new master and gain confidence. Important: Dogs have a definite rhythm of life. Therefore the puppy should have a regular daily pattern from the beginning; the times of feeding and of walking should be the same every day, as nearly as possible.

The Dog Diary: Make notes of all the important data about your dog in a notebook or book. Begin this on the first day. For example, you can note in tables and brief entries:
- the birth date
- the time you got the puppy
- date and type of inoculation and worming
- type of feed
- administration of additional vitamins and other medicines
- time and course of sicknesses or injuries
- treatment and medications dispensed

Children and Puppies: It's natural for children to want to play with puppies. A puppy should—indeed must—play too. It is used to running around with its siblings; this increases its skills and is important for the development of bones and muscles. Nevertheless, children should proceed very carefully with the little dog at first; they should not be wild or clumsy, which could be dangerous for it (see Children and Boxers, page 25). It's best if you supervise the children's play and make sure that it doesn't go on for too long. A puppy tires quickly. Then it withdraws, often quite suddenly, to its sleeping place and needs undisturbed rest. Puppies sleep many hours a day. Children don't like to see this. If you appeal to their sense of responsibility, however, they understand clearly that your little boxer is not a plaything: not a doll that you can

dress and put in the doll carriage or even bathe, and above all not a little horse that you can ride. Otherwise serious injuries to the puppy can result. It should also not be regarded as a plaything by adults or become spoiled, however much its droll expression and clumsy ways—all those things that are considered "sweet" and "cute"—invite this. It is a dog and should, despite the intimate bond with humans, be treated in accord with its primordial nature.

The First Nights

In the first nights after separation from its mother the puppy feels lonely. Each puppy responds very differently, even puppies in the same litter. You could be lucky and your new little pet may lie down peacefully in its basket and sleep quietly until morning. It could also be, however, that during the night it will howl and wail pitifully. The puppy is homesick. How is it going to get used to being alone so suddenly? Often it is not advisable to react to the puppy's complaints at all or to reprimand it energetically. I

Getting to feel at home. In the first few weeks a hot water bottle can reassure the puppy; it takes the place of the warmth of its mother.

believe it is better for you and for the boxer to give it a little help in its loneliness. You may have to sacrifice a few night hours, but it will learn to trust you at the same time and will never forget your show of love and patience. It will already be soothed if it hears your gentle voice. In addition it has proven helpful to lay a hot water bottle under the cover in the basket (a heating pad is dangerous). The hot water bottle replaces the warmth of the mother. Don't take the puppy in your arms, however, or it may try to turn this comfortable circumstance into a custom by howling constantly. Neither should it be taken into bed with you; otherwise it will always try again, perhaps for years to come, to win its place there. If your puppy howls so loudly and ceaselessly that it disturbs you and your neighbors greatly, you can take it, with its basket, into your bedroom for the first night. This way it will become quiet and soon its basket has become so comforting and beloved that you can place it in the original spot again.

Bed — The Boxer's Very Own Place

Very quickly, in about two or three days, the puppy feels at home and considers your home its home, to which it is attached and that it will later also guard. Within this home it needs its very own little domain, and that is its bed. It can withdraw there when it is tired, whenever it is sick or feels lonely, and when it has a bad conscience.

The "safe place": The right place must be found so that the puppy can feel safe, secure, and undisturbed in this refuge, a strong safe place that will not be changed. This is not so easy, for there must be no chill from the floor and no drafts. On the other hand, the immediate vicinity of a heater or stove is also bad for the well-being of the dog. Finally, when you choose a location you must

consider that the boxer is sociable, a family dog, who gladly takes part in all the goings-on. Therefore such places as a storeroom or the hallway to a cellar are unsuitable.

Before buying the bed for your boxer you can get practical advice in the pet store. There are several points you should bear in mind when making a choice.

Basket or box: A basket or a box with a flat edge or a step makes a good bed.

Lining: A basket or a box must be furnished with a lining appropriate for the season. It should be washable or at least have a washable cover.

Mattress: If you decide to use a mattress as a bed, it must be thick enough and have a sturdy, washable cover. The mattress should only be placed in a draft-free, warm place.

Size: Whether you choose box, basket, or mattress, get the size for a grown boxer, for the little puppy will quickly become a large dog. The bed should be 25 × 35 inches (65 × 90 cm) in size; better yet is a size of 27 × 39 inches (70 × 100 cm).

Warning: The bed must not be made of plastic, for if the dog chews on it and swallows a piece, this can be life threatening; this goes for foam as well, if it is not covered.

Equipment

For the puppy, as well as for the adult boxer, durable, resistant, simple equipment should be chosen.

Collar: The puppy needs a leather collar that is not too stiff. If you are afraid that your little pet may still escape, despite all precautions, have its collar furnished with a metal tag or plate on which your name, telephone number, and/or address are stamped.

The first collar will soon be too tight for the puppy. Be careful that it doesn't constrict it. Before the puppy is grown you must change the collar at least twice. Then besides its usual leather collar — which must be cleaned from time to time with saddle soap and then lightly lubricated — it can wear a chain collar. They exist in many different styles (see drawing page 23). Because the boxer is short haired and has a relatively delicate skin, the collar should not be too heavy, for it must not chafe. Collars that practically combine leather and chain have been shown to work very well (see drawing page 23). The use of the various collars that tighten when pulled — called slip or choke collars — is explained in the chapter on training (page 37). Unsuitable: are spiked collars, such as those frequently used for long-haired dogs. Training and schooling of the dog can be accomplished quite successfully without using these collars, which are often painful.

Leads: For walking in the city and for short expeditions you need the usual leather dog lead. It is about 39 inches (1 m) long and must have a strong hand loop. You also need a long lead for hiking with the dog and for training a young boxer. You can use leather reins for this, if you have them shortened, or the practical plastic leads that roll up automatically. The minimum length of this lead should be about 13 feet (4 m). Caution: The plastic lead should be held only by the grip. If you grasp the thin, strong line, a sudden tug by the dog can result in dangerous cutting off of circulation in the hand or a single finger.

Dog leads for puppies must be sturdy, for at first many puppies try to chew on the line because they want to get free. There are many leads available whose bottom end consists of a chain, which are intended to combat this bad behavior, but these are not suitable either, because the hard chain can injure delicate little teeth. A firm word from you is a better way to prevent chewing on the lead.

Food and Water Dishes: Because of its short, broad muzzle the boxer needs large dishes. They must be slide proof. Dishes of stainless steel or enameled dishes whose bottom edge has a rubber

Dog collars and leads are available in various styles. Top: Leather slip (choke) collar and chain slip collar. Center: Combined leather and chain collar. Bottom: Plastic lead with automatic roll-up, attached to a leather collar.

ring attached are therefore better than light plastic dishes. So that the dog need not bend while eating, there are dishes that are fastened in a raised holder (see drawing page 32). They must be very stable, however, so they stand really firm.

Items for Use in Care: The basic equipment for your boxer should include a brush that is not too hard, for daily brushing, and a somewhat stiffer brush for the shedding season (both with natural bristles), as well as a currycomb or rubber glove. In addition you need washcloths, to clean eyes, lips, or feet if necessary; tweezers or special tick forceps for removing ticks; and finally a small first-aid kit for dogs (see page 59).

Toys: All dogs — from puppy age on up — need and use playthings. They chew on them and bite them; they throw them and shake them back and

Maintenance and Care

forth. They satisfy their need for play and for movement. If you change the toys of the puppy frequently, its development will be promoted through many new experiences. Chewing bones and chewing rolls of buffalo hide are especially good for play because at the same time they serve to strengthen and clean the jaws. Small solid rubber balls and large rings are also appropriate playthings.

Unsuitable: are squeaky rubber toys and other items of hollow rubber. Besides the loud squeaking, which can make the dog excited and nervous, there is the danger it can swallow the rubber parts or even the metal squeaker. Also dangerous are all materials that can split, like hard plastic, celluloid, different kinds of wood, and bones (see page 26).

Working With Your Boxer

The Daily Walk

The dog must be taken out at least three times daily, often even more frequently, to relieve itself. Puppies and young dogs have this need after every meal. Under no circumstances — in spite of rain or storm, suspenseful TV film, or guests — may the walk be deferred, for the dog, which has been trained to be housebroken, will otherwise suffer torment. It's best for dog owner and dog if firm times for going out and for longer walks are set aside in the daily schedule. On walks in city districts and inner suburbs the sidewalks must not be soiled by the dog (see keeping the sidewalks clean, page 12). The dog owner is responsible for curbing the dog. On the street the dog must be kept on a lead at all times, and there are only a few parks or green areas where dogs may run free. There is a good reason for this, too, for of the many people who seek relaxation in parks, not all are dog lovers; some are even afraid of them. There is also the danger that a dog fight may develop. Besides, the dog should always remain under control so that it does not do its business in the wrong place, such as a children's playground or on a lawn.

Exercise

At least once a day the boxer should be able to let off steam with all the violence that is typical of its breed. It needs fresh air and should be exercising outside in any weather.

The boxer is quiet and is not a nervous dog, but nevertheless it conceals very high spirits. It is deceptive if the dog lies quietly for a long time in its bed or in a favorite corner, for it is only waiting for the opportunity to unleash its vitality in play or in free romping and running. Then it shows its strength, skill, and endurance. It is not only its muscular body that needs play and much exercise; its lively, alert nature requires this, too. In the first year of life its play and exercise needs are naturally especially strong. Anyone who leads a boxer for the first time will probably despair over the wild romping and running. Its exuberance can be brought under control with some patience, especially through working with the little wildling. As soon as the "storm and stress" period of the young dog is over, the boxer becomes quieter. Even then, however, it absolutely must have sufficient opportunity for play and exercise.

It's the boxer owner's fault if the dog becomes lazy and sluggish, a "couch hound," who plods tiredly and heavily beside its master on weak legs and with bloated body. A properly maintained boxer can have tension in its body and elasticity in its movements until the end of its life. There are even "boxer senior citizens" that take part in dog trials with joy and competitive spirit.

Play at Home and Outside

The boxer will play alone with a toy for only a short time. Play is really interesting if it can share it with a two-legged or a four-legged companion. At home and on walks it never fails to encourage play. It brings its ball or, if you are out in the country, a stick or a branch and waits for you to toss the object so it can spring after it and bring it back to you. Here is a good opportunity for you to work in some training of the dog (see page 24). For a city dweller who would like to offer its dog purposeful exercise and a free run, the best chance is the dog training ground or the country outing. Since this is only rarely possible on a daily basis, the workout and exciting play with the dog at any opportunity that offers, even in the house, are very important.

What you must keep in mind when playing: The favorite game of the dog — running after and finding a thrown object — should not be started too young, in contrast to other games and first training practices. In my experience, some boxers who become used to this game as a puppy later run after everything that moves and worry it, from butterflies to cattle. Therefore it's best to hold off with this game until the young dog has learned the basic rules of obedience.

Be careful when playing outdoors that your boxer does not carry split, crumbling, or rotten branches (sticks without bark are best). Don't let it pick up stones, either. There are boxers that have a liking for stones and will even carry large field stones wedged in wide-open jaws for long distances, if they are not hindered. Stones are

Retrieving. The boxer must learn to find an object its master has thrown as quickly as possible and to bring it back.

bad for the jaws of the dog; the teeth may be ground off. Some dogs, especially puppies and young dogs, have the dangerous tendency to eat small stones. Neither stern words nor punishment helps against this. The cause of this behavior is usually a disorder of the metabolism or of the intestinal flora. Therefore it's best to consult the veterinarian.

The Boxer in the Yard

A yard offers your boxer the ideal "playground," as long as ornamental shrubbery, flower beds, and vegetable gardens do not inhibit its movements. If plantings have to be protected, an unused part of the yard, some 60 to 120 square yards (50–100 m^2), can be made into an exercise area by the addition of fencing, a gate, and a shelter. Strong fencing and the elements for do-it-yourself assembly of a solid wooden shelter are available from special firms whose addresses you will find in the publications of the dog clubs. Of course it's also fun to build the house yourself, and wire fencing can be used for the run. The enclosure must be high and strong, however, if you want to be sure that your dog will remain inside the fence. That goes for the grounds themselves, too. Boxers can leap extraordinarily high, so the normal high fence is no barrier to them when possessed by the urge for freedom. The bottom of the fence should be sunk into the ground so that your boxer cannot dig itself a little escape hole, which boxers love to do.

Be sure that it always has enough water in its enclosure. A family dog should not be left in the yard overnight.

Children and Boxers

For parents it is a nice but not always easy task to teach their children the proper way to treat a boxer without sacrificing the children's lack of inhibition. It is important that children learn early to behave patiently and as firmly as possible with the dog and that they are ready to make small sacrifices for it. The responsibility for the dog and its behavior always belongs to the parents, not the children.

The boxer is known as a lover of children, and rightly so, but this should not lead to the neglect of some important rules:

● Small children and infants must not be left alone with the boxer without supervision, for this can — in rare cases — result in dangerous situations because of its violent play or its protective instincts.

● Care must be taken when children play with puppies: the puppies can bite and scratch badly.

● Parents should be sure that the dog, especially in the puppy stage, is not treated by the children as a playmate and is also not used as a plaything.

● Children must know that they may not anger, frighten, or hurt the dog; they must not hit it, or pinch it, or pull on its ears, tail, or tender lips.

● Children should not disturb the boxer when it is sleeping or eating.

● Children should not walk the boxer alone. It is too strong for them, and they could not hold it if the need arose. This could be dangerous.

● Children must be made aware that dogs behave differently outdoors and that they are guided differently and react differently from the way they do in the house.

● Children should be careful with strange dogs; they should not be as trusting with them as with their own; they must be especially careful with chained dogs; these can snap or bite because they function as watchdogs.

● Children should never intervene in a fight or when dogs are biting. They should call an adult for help if the dogs don't separate from one another by themselves.

● After play and work with the dog, children should wash their hands and brush their nails; they should not allow the dog to lick them, even if the danger of infection is very small because of inoculations and worming.

Dangers in the House, on the Street, and in the Woods

Before your boxer comes to its new home for the first time, there are all kinds of precautions to take to avoid possible accidents.

In the house, for example, uncovered electric wires must be out of the new arrival's reach until you are absolutely certain that it won't chew on them; this could mean its death. Foam and plastic can also be dangerous to your dog. Also cotton, plastic bags, and any kind of chemical material, especially mouse and rat poison, must not be where your dog can get it. Great danger is also posed by nails, small pins, and needles. Next it is advisable to examine the neighborhood and the yard.

Street traffic brings with it many dangers for the boxer, especially for puppies, young dogs, and all dogs without training. Happily the proper behavior for the street is easy to instill in the intelligent boxer. On a busy street and at all crossings, however, the dog should be on a lead. An obedient dog that dependably follows all commands can accompany its master on a quiet suburban or country road without being on the lead. It is immediately released on meeting other dogs, however, and in the country cats or chickens can incite it to chase them. Therefore it's up to your own judgment how much freedom you can allow it.

In woods and fields the same is true. Unfortunately it's not true, as is very often said, that boxers neither hunt nor harry. Every dog carries in it the urge to hunt. Depending on the breed and the individual circumstances of the dog, this urge expresses itself very differently. It is important to be aware that your boxer, especially as a young dog, is not "taught" by other comrades and induced to harry. As soon as a dog is found out of the control of its master in woods and fields of certain locales, the hunter is legally permitted to kill the animal. This measure, which fortunately very seldom needs to be carried out, appears extremely severe. Whoever knows the gruesome behavior of wild dogs can understand this law, however. The responsibility for the killing of a dog by a hunter is born by the dog owner. The danger of rabies infection continues, in spite of countless measures to combat this deadly disease. Regular immunization shots are the only practical defense against it.

Small Outings and Long Trips with the Boxer

When longer outings and big trips are planned the question arises: what to do with the dog? Puppies and young dogs should not be left alone, for any change in their life-style can have a negative effect. Even the adult boxer suffers greatly during separation from its master and would rather endure the stress of a journey than be apart. Therefore the best thing to do is to take it along with you.

Rides and Outings in the Car

Almost all boxers like to ride in the car. Before the journey starts the dog should have a not very large meal and should be walked so that it can relieve itself. Its place is always in the back part of the car. Since the seats have a bend slightly toward the rear, the dog must lie crosswise, which on long journeys is very uncomfortable for the animal. You can give it a level bed by means of a folding cover. Firms specializing in dog equipment, whose addresses you can find in dog fanciers' journals, supply covers that assure the dog of a healthy position and protect the seat. On each trip be sure:

● that your boxer gets fresh air, without being in a draft.

● that there is always fresh water along for it.

● that every two hours or so you provide a little stop so your dog can relieve itself; near highways it should always be on a lead for safety's sake.

● that the dog is never left in the heat. Boxers, like almost all dogs, suffer in heat. This becomes noticeable very quickly during car trips in the summer: The dog becomes more and more exhausted and panting. Therefore stop, if possible where there is some water — a brook, river, pond, or lake — to give the dog a chance to refresh itself and cool off.

Waiting in the car: If you must park the car for a long time, without being able to take the dog with you, you should be especially considerate of its well-being. In moderate temperatures it can stay in the car alone without harm for a while, so long as a supply of air is available through a window opening. As soon as it becomes warm, however, the sun shines on the car and the heat inside the car increases; staying there is unbearable for the dog. It's also bad for the dog if it must wait in a cold car for a long time. In any event the dog should not be left in parking garages above or below ground, for there the concentration of exhaust can be harmful and even dangerous.

With the Boxer on Vacation

If you want to take your boxer on an overnight journey or an even longer trip, you can avoid possible difficulties by good planning and preparation. First, find out what inns, motels, and hotels take dogs. You can get the appropriate lists through automobile clubs. For trips out of the country you must observe all the pertinent rules.

Traveling equipment for your boxer should include the following:

● short and long leads, collar with address tag

● brushes and tweezers

● food dish, water dish, and favorite toy

● food supplies (dry complete meals), depending on the possibility of getting food while you are on the way and at your destination

● a small traveling supply of medications (your veterinarian can tell you which medications you

Maintenance and Care

should take and which additional calcium tablets if you tell him or her where you are going)

• a firm sleeping surface is very important

Next you should make sure: When your boxer must be left alone in a hotel room for the first time, return to the room after a short time to find out whether it barks, howls, or chews on any of the furniture. In such a case, try with patience and firmness, perhaps even with treats, to get it used to the new quarters.

Some boxers react to climate and food changes with lassitude or intestinal upsets. If the condition of the dog does not improve very soon, you should find a veterinarian.

Trips by Train, Ship, or Airplane: It's best to find out from your travel agent or directly from the railroad, airline, or shipping line about arrangements for the transport of the dog. Costs and requirements are different. For airplane flights your boxer must ride in a special transport cage in the freight hold of the airplane. This kind of imprisonment is mostly a torment for the dog, as it is also for a long journey by sea, despite tranquilizers that can be administered by your veterinarian. Therefore in such cases it is better for your boxer if you avoid taking it with you, always assuming that you can leave it well cared for at home.

Care While You Are Away

Relatives, friends or neighbors are best to care for your boxer while you are away. They already know the dog and it trusts them and doesn't feel strange. Give them its usual equipment — basket, food dishes, and toys — and a feeding schedule, and the separation will be easier for it.

The breeder or the family from whom you got the dog could also be asked if they might take care of it while you are away. It would then certainly be well looked after.

A good vacation home for your dog might also be located through a newspaper ad. There are many people who cannot have a dog but would gladly take care of an animal for a short period. Obviously you must make sure ahead of time whether your boxer will be looked after lovingly and correctly there.

A boarding kennel is another possibility for the care of your boxer. There as a rule dogs are very well looked after. Unfortunately there are also exceptions. Ultimately it is a matter of trust when you must leave your dog in the care of others.

The Care of the Boxer

Coat Care: Lots of Brushing — Little Bathing

The boxer's coat should be smooth and shining. This is a sign of good health but also evidence of basic coat care.

The daily brushing is regarded by most boxers as a kindness. It massages the skin and stirs the circulation, which is especially important at shedding time. A sturdy brush with natural bristles, especially a curry brush, is best for coat care. For puppies, young dogs, and boxers with sensitive skin, a gentle, soft brush is used. Also, it's better to brush the head of the dog with a softer brush. The boxer coat becomes especially full and shining if you brush it once against the grain, then strongly with the grain, and you finish by rubbing it with a damp chamois. Use this chamois also to carefully clean its head and remove dust from the folds.

Bathing your boxer is necessary only in exceptional circumstances, if you groom it daily. Aside from the fact that bathing usually becomes a difficult and damp procedure, washing a dog with soap and water is bad for the important natural oil secretions of the skin.

Maintenance and Care

<u>Puppies</u> should not be bathed under any circumstances. Their soft skin can be kept clean with good brushing. Dirty spots can be cleaned with lukewarm water and a sponge or piece of chamois.

<u>Adult dogs</u> who are following a primordial instinct and now and again roll in offal or feces can only be cleaned by a thorough bath. Use a dog shampoo from the pet store. Most boxers allow themselves to be placed in the bathtub very unwillingly. It's best if you leave the collar on your dog to begin with so that you can hold it fast and the dog can't jump out of the bathtub soaking wet. In any case it's better to wear a rubber apron or something like it. The body and the legs are thoroughly washed with lukewarm water and shampoo, the head washed only with water: Be careful not to get water or soap into the ears! When the coat is well rinsed, it's best if you wrap your dog in a large, old bath towel and lift it out of the tub in the towel. Then it can shake itself hard without its spraying everywhere. The dog should not be allowed to be in any draft before it is entirely dry.

Caution: If, while brushing or bathing, you discover a flea, louse, or mite infestation, institute an attack on the parasites immediately (see page 58).

Examination and Care of the Eyes and Ears

The Eyes: The boxer has large eyes; sometimes they even protrude a little. In contrast to many other breeds of dog they are little protected by lashes or skin. This therefore leads easily to irritation, infection, or small wounds. As soon as you notice an eye tearing, the eyelid swelling, or an inflamed eyeball, you must take your boxer to the veterinarian. Many boxers have morning "sleep" in their eyes. This is entirely normal. It is merely a small secretion in the corners of the eyes, which can be wiped away with a clean, damp, nonlinty cloth; you can also clean the bridge of the nose at the same time.

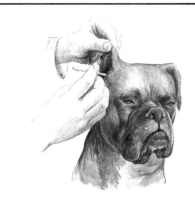

Cleaning the outer ears must be undertaken carefully with a cotton swab. <u>Do not probe inside the ear canal.</u>

The Ears: Cropped ears require minimal care. Only the external, visible part of the ear should be cleaned very carefully. Use a cotton swab and an ear cleanser recommended by the veterinarian. Infrequent cleaning is healthier for the dog than doing it too often.

If you observe that your boxer frequently holds its head at an angle, shakes it, and acts as if moving its ears is painful, or if you smell an unusual odor inside the ear, immediately take it to the veterinarian. An ear infection is the cause of the complaint, and it must be treated at once.

Tooth Care

A properly nourished boxer almost always has a strong, healthy set of teeth.

For cleaning the teeth and for protection against tartar buildup your boxer should be given dog biscuits or hard bread daily as well as buffalo hide bones to chew on now and again. On principle it should not be allowed to have sweets, since they are bad for its teeth.

Because some dogs have a tendency to tartar buildup and since other tooth ailments or infections of the gums can crop up, you should inspect your boxer's jaws from time to time. To do so, carefully open the jaws: one hand grasps the upper jaw; the other carefully pulls down the lower jaw.

Tartar shows as a yellowish deposit. It can be removed with a cotton swab or a small toothbrush saturated with lemon juice. If thorough cleaning of the teeth is unsuccessful, the veterinarian must help. Untreated tartar can lead to infection. This is indicated by an unusual, foul odor. Infected roots and lost teeth can result.

Examination and Care of the Feet

The boxer is one dog that absolutely must have exercise; it wants and needs to run a great deal. Its feet must stay strong and healthy.

After long walks or hikes you should carefully examine its feet. All kinds of foreign bodies can become stuck between the toes and must be removed. They cause pain; they can also lead to swelling, infection, and small wounds. In many cases the dog cures it by licking it itself. If improvement does not appear after a short time, however, you should take it to the veterinarian.

In winter the feet must be cared for especially carefully. Many streets and sidewalks are spread with salt. Dogs suffer from it; the soles or pads become dry and cracked. The tiny grains of the salt can even cut the dog's foot. You protect your boxer against all these influences if before every walk you rub around the pads of its foot with petroleum jelly. After the walk the foot can be washed in lukewarm water, dried, and the lubricant gently rubbed in once again. This keeps the skin elastic.

Regular care of the claws is usually only necessary for dogs that move very little or that run mainly on soft surfaces, such as grass or carpets. The claws of dogs that are allowed to spend a great deal of time outdoors wear down by themselves. Shortening the claws should only be done by those who are experienced or should be left to the veterinarian.

Worming and Inoculations

Healthy, well-maintained, properly nourished boxers are not very susceptible to parasites and infectious illnesses. Nevertheless, part of the responsible care of the dog is the provision of protective shots and the occasional worming.

If you have a suspicion that your boxer has worms (see page 16), the dog's feces should be examined by the veterinarian so that he or she can, if necessary, prescribe special medication. Worming should not be undertaken under any circumstances if the dog is in a stress situation, such as travel, illness, or change of residence or owner.

Please pay close attention to all the inoculation dates after the basic immunization (see immunization, page 58).

Proper Feeding — A Healthy Diet

The Feeding Place

Like its sleeping place, the boxer's feeding place also belongs to its own little domain and should be appropriately set up at the very beginning. Appropriately means that the dog has enough space to eat its food unhindered and comfortably. For example, some dogs like to set aside a large piece of meat so that they can enjoy eating it while lying down. It is thus practical to put a washable protective cover beneath the bowls unless the floor underneath is tile. It's not unusual for boxers, with their wide muzzle, to strew little bits of food around the bowl, so food and water dishes should be as large as possible (see page 23).

Feeding Times

Regular feeding times and the number of meals appropriate to the age of the dog are essential for the dog's good development and health. As a general rule it follows that:

Puppies from 8 to 12 weeks need five meals a day: morning, midmorning, midday, afternoon, and evening.

Puppies from three months to the end of the change of teeth (five to six months) require four meals: morning, early midday, afternoon, and early evening.

Young dogs from six months on get three meals: morning, midday, and afternoon; as the dog develops, the midday meal can be omitted, so that by the age of one-and-a-half to two years only two meals are necessary — in the morning and in early afternoon.

The adult dog from about two years old needs only one meal daily. This can be given in the period between late morning and early afternoon. Between meals it may have a dog biscuit or some hard bread.

Food Quantities

The quantity of food for your boxer varies according to
- age
- size
- duties it must perform
- digestion
- season
- individual eating habits

The quantity will therefore not be the same for all.

As a general rule: If there is something left in the bowl after the end of a meal, the quantity is too

Average Food Quantities

Age	Weight	Damp food	Dry food
2 mo	13.23 lb. (6 kg)	28.0 oz (800 g)	8.4 oz (240 g)
2½ mo	22.00 lb (10 kg)	31.5 oz (900 g)	9.1 oz (260 g)
7 mo	44.00 lb (20 kg)	38.5 oz (1100 g)	12.25 oz (350 g)
12 mo	85.98 lb (39 kg)	49.0 oz (1400 g)	14.70 oz (420 g)

The quantities listed in the table are considered maintenance quantities. The amounts needed for stress conditions (during growth, pregnancy and lactation, training, or other strenuous circumstances) are so varied that the food quantities must be measured according to your own experience.

31

Proper Feeding — A Healthy Diet

Food bowls whose height is adjustable are comfortable for the boxer, since it need not bend way down; however, they should not be set too high.

large. If your boxer empties its bowl and then keeps licking thoroughly, the quantity was too small. Since most dogs do not have the same appetite at all times, you should observe how much your boxer eats. At the same time observe whether it becomes thinner or gains weight. You can tell this best by looking at its ribs: they should not be too noticeably visible under the fur but should be easy to feel with your hand.

If you are still uncertain about the quantity of food, you can judge by the scientifically determined average values.

Food Composition and Ingredients

The food for your boxer must be correct; that is, it must contain all the required nutrients and building materials and should be mixed so that the dog's digestion can handle it. Healthy natural feed for your boxer consists of fresh, good-quality meat as the basic food, with the addition of vegetable material in the form of grain prod-

ucts as well as vegetables and fruit as supplementary foods. Vitamin and mineral supplements are added.

Meat

Meat guarantees the important protein supply for the dog. Depending on the dog's age, it's best if the meat is raw and cut in small pieces (such as chopped meat or cubed meat). Raw meat contains valuable nutrients that can be greatly diminished in the process of cooking. The worry that fresh meat can make a dog snappish or mean is unfounded, and an unpleasant smell from the throat has other causes than the enjoyment of raw meat. Meat inspection in this country guarantees that fresh meat is free of salmonella, tapeworms, and trichina. (Be careful in foreign countries — use prepared food or cooked meat!) There are dogs who get used to cooked meat as puppies and later eat no raw meat or eat it only if they are very hungry. For these dogs the meat can be cooked in a little water, and then the broth, with the nutrients still in it, can be given along with the food.

Muscle meat: Of the various kinds of meat, beef is the most nourishing and most digestible. For a change the dog can also be fed mutton (without fat), wild animal meat, and poultry.

Fish: The protein-rich flesh of fish is very popular with many boxers. Fish must be carefully prepared, however, to be really free of bones, which are very dangerous for your boxer.

Caution: Raw pork can be very, very dangerous for our four-legged friends and should never be fed to them. It can contain viruses that cause Aujeszky's disease (Pseudorabies), an incurable infectious illness which doesn't pose a threat to human health. Cooked pork, which has a high fat content, is poorly suited to the boxer.

Organ meats

Besides the mostly quite expensive muscle meats the various innards are good nourishment, either as basic food or as supplements.

Proper Feeding — A Healthy Diet

Green tripe is the uncleaned, raw first stomach of cattle. It contains the still partially digested remains of green fodder and therefore comes closest to the primordial nourishment for the dog. This nutrient-rich food is unfortunately very hard to get and has a very strong smell, which serves as a further disadvantage.

White tripe, cleaned and scalded, which is available from many butchers, cannot be used as a basic food because its nutrient value has decreased; it may only be used as a supplement or for a change.

Liver and kidneys are filtering organs and can contain toxic materials. They should be given to the dog only from time to time, when they should be "detoxified," the kidneys by soaking in water and the liver by soaking in milk for a number of hours. Basically the blood-building, vitamin-rich liver is a valuable source of nourishment, especially if it is fed raw. In some dogs it produces diarrhea, however (liver has a purging effect; see Constipation, page 60).

Spleen and udder also have a purgative effect. They are used only as occasional food supplements.

Lungs should not be used at all because of their small food value.

Canned meat: see Commercial Dog Food, page 33.

Vegetable Foods

These fill the need for carbohydrates; therefore they are an important component of the diet.

Grain products exist in the form of commercial kibble and rolled oats as well as rice and cornmeal (both used cooked); soy flour can also be used for nourishment.

Almost all kinds of vegetables are suitable, with the exception of cabbage and legumes.

Fruit, such as apples, pears, and bananas, is fed raw; citrus fruit is fed as juice.

Caution: Cherries, plums, and other stone fruits should not be used because of the pits.

Supplementary Food

Other foods increase and enrich the diet. Especially good is skim milk cottage cheese, which contains many animal proteins and now and again can be substituted for a meal of meat; furthermore, eggs (about two a week: the yolk raw, the white cooked) and milk (especially for the growing dog) and also chopped herbs and garlic are occasionally good for boxers. Hard bread is not only good for the dog's teeth but also for the digestion and is rich in carbohydrates. Finally, the dog needs a certain amount of fat, in winter more than in summer. The fat contained in meat does not always meet the fat requirement, especially not for growing and working dogs. A small addition of sunflower or wheat germ oil is a good idea (unless you are already using a cod-liver oil supplement).

Vitamins and Minerals

Vitamins, minerals, and trace elements are necessary for the health of the dog. If you mix the food fresh yourself, you should add the missing supplements. The choice of the right preparations and the correct dosage are important; both must be appropriate to the age and condition of your dog. Tablets that combine all the important vitamins and minerals in the proper proportions are very good. Ask your veterinarian for advice. You can usually get the necessary preparations from the veterinarian; otherwise you can buy them in a pet store or in some drugstores.

Cod-liver oil, in the right dosage, is a valuable aid to general strength in the wintertime. Give your boxer a teaspoon in the feed two times a week in the winter and a half teaspoon two times a week in transition periods.

Commercial Dog Food

If you feed your boxer ready-made dog food, all the important basic elements are supplied in a calibrated mixture. It is scientifically developed

Proper Feeding — A Healthy Diet

and tested, and the product is constantly inspected. Its great advantage is in the saving of time, which is gained through faster preparation. An important additional point is that on a trip the dog can be fed easily and with food of guaranteed quality. If you ever must board your boxer while you are away, your friends or neighbors will be grateful for the easy feeding. Therefore get your puppy used to eating prepared food, even if you primarily use fresh food. Now and then it should be given commercial food as a treat or as a reward.

Prepared food is available in the store in cans or in packages in many varieties. Since the "tastes" of dogs are also different, do not be discouraged if your dog doesn't like one brand or eats only reluctantly; it will probably like another very much.

Important: When using commercially prepared food, look for the manufacturing date when you buy it and use the recommended quantities of the food.

It is very important that the water dish stand beside the food dish and be kept filled with fresh water. The dog's need for fluid is especially high with dry food. If you give your boxer alternately fresh food and prepared food or supplement one with the other, pay attention to the proportions of the protein, nutrients, vitamins, and minerals. If you are not certain, your veterinarian can also advise you in this case.

Practical Advice for Feeding

● Make a feeding plan for your dog.
● Stock the necessary food ahead of time, if you can store it appropriately; you will save time and money this way.
● Get your boxer accustomed from the first day forward to eating what you give it, even fruit, vegetables, calcium, and vitamin tablets.

Rules for Feeding
● Make sure that your boxer always has fresh water at its feeding place.
● Mix the feed in the correct proportions: one-third meat, two-thirds vegetable material (chiefly kibble, to which some vegetables and/or fruit has been added).
● Make the food medium firm, that is, not watery or soupy, but also not too dry.
● Give the food lukewarm, if possible — never hot and never directly out of the refrigerator!
● Spices are indigestible; salt, on the other hand, the dog may and should have (half a knifetip per fresh meal).
● Let your boxer eat completely undisturbed and also let it rest after the meal.
● Clean the food bowl after every meal.
● Make sure that your boxer doesn't overeat if it is hungry. If it tends to fat (older dogs), make one day a week a fast day on which it receives only water.
● If your boxer often lacks appetite, although its health is good, make a change in its menu.

Unsuitable Food
● Do not feed your boxer leftovers; they do not offer the proper nourishment.
● Do not get it used to sweets. They are indigestible, ruin its teeth, and induce saliva flow. As a treat use a piece of dog biscuit or some bread spread with lightly spiced sausage.
● Never give your boxer food from the table, and see to it that others do not. It not only accustoms it to begging, but also it begins to "slobber" (see page 55).
● Avoid giving bones to your dog. Boxers tend to gulp and then can easily strangle. Poultry bones are especially dangerous, because like all splintery bones they can cause internal injuries.

Boxers miming. Top: Two boxers with extraordinary facial expressions. Bottom: Posture of expectation — in some boxers this is mixed with mistrust.

Training and Obedience Training

Steps in Training

A puppy is ready to be removed from its mother as soon as it begins boldly and curiously to explore its environment. When it is separated from her and comes to its new master, the master takes on the responsibility for the little creature and, to protect it, must begin training right away. The unsuspecting puppy now faces an extensive learning program.

Importance of training: What your boxer learns in the first six months of its life imprints its character and is the basis for its further development. Its education should be built up in steps and must be followed through as consistently as possible. An omission in the training of the puppy or young dog can scarcely be made good again and brings many a problem over the course of the years.

The "pack leader": It's best if the family members agree at the beginning about who will take the responsibility for the training and become the "pack leader" for the new little arrival. For the puppy the family is now a pack with an order of ranking, to which it submits. It recognizes the strongest as leader. Obviously the other family members also indirectly take part in the training procedures. They should proceed in the same way as the "pack leader," however. If several people train the puppy, this can induce behavioral disturbances. Thus it is also very important that all use the same commands.

Training. Top: To jump over a barrier the boxer must exhibit daring, strength, and skill. Bottom: The boxer's body is powerfully muscled; its movements are elastic. (This is the three-year-old Meikel von Nassau-Oranien.)

Housebreaking must be begun early. At the beginning and in emergencies a newspaper can be used as the "appointed place."

The First Steps

The puppy must climb all the initial important learning steps on the ladder to becoming a well-trained dog at the same time: becoming housebroken, walking on a lead, and coming when called. Thus, learning obedience is part of the training. Since the boxer is especially quick and eager to learn, teacher and pupil usually have an easy time with one another. Naturally each puppy has its own character and its individual temperament; this gives variety to the training period. However, with kindness, much patience, and — which is usually the most difficult — consistency even the most independent little boxer can be trained.

Ground Rules for Training: This applies to all the steps of training: much praise, little punishment, and no blows. Punishment or deprivation must always directly follow the transgression; otherwise the dog cannot grasp the connection between crime and punishment.

Training and Obedience Training

Housebreaking

Basically the puppy has to relieve itself upon waking and after every meal. This is every two to three hours during the day; during the night it can hold out for about six to seven hours. The first few days are therefore a little strenuous because of the many walks that have to be taken, but it pays to take the trouble: the more consistent you are, the more quickly the puppy will be housebroken.

Many breeders make sure that the puppy is already housebroken before they let it go. In this case you should pay careful attention to how and when it makes its needs known and then take it out right away. It shows its need when it sniffs the floor and turns itself around. Then it is high time to set the puppy in an appointed place to which it should also accustom itself. If you have a yard, find a suitable "regular place" for it. It can go quickly or it may take some time until the puppy has done its business; in any case it must be praised with an appreciative "good dog" afterward. On the street it is not so simple to find the right place for it, since it may use only the curb, to which you must accustom it (see Keeping the Sidewalk Clean, page 12).

If you have no opportunity to let the puppy run free, you can make do with newspapers at first. Spread out several pages in various places, and place the puppy on them as soon as it begins to make preparations to go. Then lay the bottommost page of the used newspaper on top of a new one so that the little dog recognizes its place by the smell the next time.

A little accident: Should your puppy have an accident — which in the beginning is almost unavoidable — and you notice it immediately afterward, say a strong "No!" If you only find the puddle or the bowel movement sometime later, the admonition will no longer help.

After cleaning, the spots made by a puppy must be rubbed further with a disinfectant, ammonia, or vinegar so that it won't use that spot again. Larger puppies are able to hold out for a longer time and make their needs known by various noises or scratching at the door in time.

Leading on a Leash

On the first walk you must take your puppy on a lead. This is a new, strange feeling for the little boxer, when it can no longer run free, as it has until now, but must move on a lead at the will of another creature. Most puppies soon become accommodated to the unfamiliar restraint; they are eager to learn and quickly find pleasure in running along beside the master like a big well-behaved boxer. There are, however, some puppies that very strongly resist the unfamiliar curtailment of their freedom. They balk, bite the lead, brace their strong, little legs against the movement, try to sit down, or strain in the opposite direction. In this case only patience will help. Violent pulling or dragging increases the resistance or frightens the little boxer. You will meet the protest most effectively through soothing talk and with much praise as soon as the little rebel has moved several steps forward. This first obedience practice should take place in the yard or in the apartment for the first time — never, ever on the busy street.

The Lead Hand: Accustom your dog from the beginning to walk on your left side. The left hand is the lead hand so that your right hand remains free.

Exception: On the right sidewalk of a street where traffic is particularly heavy, the dog should be led on the right to avoid possible hazards. It must also walk on the right side when accompanying a bicycle rider.

Calling Your Dog

Choosing a Name: Short, easily remembered names are the best, since they ease the training and the effect on the dog. Boxers are alert and curious. They quickly get used to a new name. Call your puppy for the first few days, using only the new name, when it is going to be fed or when you want to play with it or take it out. It will thus soon associate the name with pleasant experiences and obey willingly as soon as it hears the new name. Afterward praise the intelligent little dog and call it by name in an appreciative tone of voice.

The Command "Come": If your puppy will not obey because it is playing or diverted, or perhaps because it has a particularly independent character, you must not give in. Even the very youngest dog quickly notices that you've let it get away with something and will try from then on to get its own way at any opportunity. As "pack leader" you must now energetically and consistently demand obedience of the little dog; of course this is done with the command "come" and using its name. If necessary use a clap with a folded newspaper on its behind or, better, just beside it — both have the same effect.

Following Without a Lead: You can avoid small and large hazards or vexations if your boxer obeys this basic obedience practice, the command to follow. As soon as your puppy has learned to walk willingly on the lead and responds to its name, you can try letting it run free in a quiet, danger-free, supervised open stretch. It should then remain on your left side. Probably, however, it will go its own way and run away. Now call it by name, coaxingly at first; if it doesn't obey, use a firm "come," but never run after it. It will only feel pursued or will regard the whole thing as a game, like those it played with its littermates. Go along in the same direction for a little way, if necessary with faster or heavier steps, and it will probably very soon follow you — out of either curiosity or anxiety. It has now earned praise, which at the same time works to train it. If the exploring puppy does not come back right away, tempt it with a treat, which you always have handy for such an occasion. It sometimes demands patience and a little imagination as well to teach the lively, playful puppy to obey, but this is the only way it can be trained to be dependable and obedient.

The dog whistle: A good resource to which your boxer should become accustomed early is the dog whistle. For long distances you can use a "soundless" dog whistle. The pitch of this whistle is so high that the dog can hear it but humans can't (see hearing, page 50).

The Important Obedience Exercise "Sit"

An exercise that the dog learns easily is sitting. For this we use the command "sit." You can convey the meaning of this short, precise word to your puppy in a simple way: With one hand holds its head high and gently press its rear end with the other until the puppy sits. While you are doing this, say slowly and impressively, "sit," stroke it — that is, praise it with the word "good." The sitting position is only maintained briefly when it is an obedience exercise. The puppy should remain in position for a moment. If you then call it with an approving "come" or

"Sit" is taught the dog by drawing its head into an upright position with the lead in one hand; at the same time the rear end is pressed down with the other hand.

with its name, the puppy will joyfully leap toward you and thus demonstrate that this exercise has been a lot of fun for it.

Important: The command "sit" is important in the following situations:

- at a red light
- before crossing a street
- waiting in front of a store (leashed!) or in another situation where it must wait for awhile
- when your boxer is about to greet someone violently and jump
- when it wants to chase cats, chickens, or wild animals

In all such situations the best security comes from stopping the dog in its tracks with the command "sit."

At Feeding: Your boxer will exhibit unusual self-control if you accustom it, as early as possible, to wait, sitting, before its filled food dish until you give it a sign to "take" so that it can begin its meal.

Staying in Its Bed

Early on, even as a puppy, your dog must learn to lie in its bed and to wait there until it is called again. This is preparation for the command "down" (see page 41), which is part of the puppy's later training. Since it is not pleasing to a puppy or a young dog to be compelled to leave its play and other kinds of activity to rest quietly in its basket, it is best if you begin this little-liked exercise when the puppy is already tired. Take it to the basket with a firm "down" or "go to bed." If it doesn't lie down there on its own, carefully draw its front legs forward and watch to see that it doesn't get up again. This place is its own domain, of course, to which it gladly withdraws — and the older the dog gets, the more frequently it will do so.

Caution: Your boxer should not feel punished if it is sent to its basket. Do not forget to "release" it again, either, after a measured time; you do this with a summoning "come" and praise it at the same time.

Staying Alone

An extremely important point in the education of a dog is getting used to being alone occasionally. Anyone who is compelled to take a dog everywhere because otherwise the abandoned animal will wreak harm and havoc becomes a slave to the four-legged friend and must miss out on much. As early as possible the puppy or young dog should become comfortable with the completely new circumstance of being alone. Leave the puppy alone — best if it is tired — for a brief period at first, and observe whether it remains quiet. If it whimpers, howls, or barks, scratches at the door, or begins to chew on its basket, go back and talk with it kindly, without punishing it. Practice leaving it alone every day. The puppy will quickly become used to this, and you can leave it alone for longer periods from time to time. There are, of course, young dogs that always scratch on doors or in their despairing circumstances gnaw and bite. A firm "no" or "shame" and possibly a loud blow with a folded newspaper on the chewed item or the scratched door are the right ways to get the dog out of this bad habit.

"Heel" and "Down"

The obedience exercises "heel" and "down" are somewhat more difficult for the dog than the first behavior lessons that he learns.

Heel: The dog walks at the left side of the master at the same tempo that the master uses, but at no time does the dog press ahead of the master: its head should never be farther forward than your left knee. Practice with the dog on the lead at first, with the lead held somewhat slackly. For very temperamental dogs the slip or choke collar (see page 23) is used. It must be placed correctly (see illustration below) and also should, even after a short tug, free the neck again by loosening the choke; otherwise injury could result. It can be a help in the exercise if you let the dog walk between you and a house wall or a fence so that it can't break out to the side. You can combat the

Training and Obedience Training

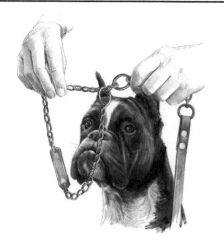

The slip collar must be so placed that the chain slides easily toward the side of the leading hand.

The boxer may not:
- beg
- rip, chew, or scratch anything
- lie on beds or upholstered furniture
- jump on people
- bark without reason
- pull on the lead
- dig in the yard
- roam and fight

attempt to hurry ahead if you wave a branch or a switch back and forth in front of its head once in a while. Admonish it continually with a firm "heel." As soon as it masters this exercise, it must learn to heel without a lead and of course on straight stretches as well as curves.

The Exercise "Down": If your boxer has already learned to stay in its bed (see page 40), you can very quickly teach it the exercise "down" out of doors. As soon as you give the command "down," it should lie down ("lie down and lie still") and not get up until you call it with "here." Then it must come as quickly as possible.

What a Well-Trained Boxer May Not Do

If the young dog has learned in many lessons what it should do, it must also at the same time learn what it must not do.

The Begging Dog Is a Tempted Dog

A dog will not beg if it never receives anything edible except what it gets at feeding time (see page 31). If you hold strictly to this rule and never get it used to "extra portions," you are never subject to the pleading looks of your boxer and it will neither beg nor have undesirable drooling. Also it will remain quiet in restaurants or pubs and not try to hunt up something at other tables.

Expensive Bad Habits: Biting, Chewing, and Scratching

It's more difficult than inhibiting begging to train a young, playful, and energetic boxer not to bite, chew, and scratch. It will try it out once to see how far it can push its play. You yourself must set the limits firmly and unmistakably: at first try distracting it. For example, if it is chewing on a shoe, take the shoe away from it with a firm "no" and instead give it the buffalo hide bone. Another example: If the dog scratches on the carpet, since it cannot know that this jolly work causes damage and is forbidden, admonish it in a loud, reproachful voice and give it a rubber ball to play with or take it for a walk. If, as is usually the case, it begins to scratch again, it must be given a smack with a newspaper. This may take some time and costs nerve and patience and may also result in some damage before the young dog has learned what is permitted and what is forbidden.

Training and Obedience Training

The Boxer Does Not Belong on Furniture or Beds

Something that every dog especially loves is lying on upholstered furniture and beds. Should your boxer try to lie on furniture or beds against your will, shoo it off with a strong admonition or clapping. However, see if there is any basis for its persistence, such as the floor being cold. In this case simply place its basket on a wooden platform made by the carpenter or on a flat box; it must be firmly mounted, however. Another possibility is for you to give your boxer an old chair, placed somewhere where it won't disturb you. The dog may then sit there and in no other chair.

Tiresome Jumping

A very troublesome habit many boxers have is that of jumping. Particularly at a moment of greeting, it is often simply not possible to keep the excited dog in check. Jumping is, of course, an expression of joy and love, which now must be rejected. Based on my own personal experience I suggest that when your dog joyfully greets your arrival by jumping (or welcomes guests this way), don't turn this expression of love aside with scolding, or even with blows. Instead, hold it for a moment, bend down to it, praise it, and calm it and tell it emphatically, "don't jump." If you repeat this at every similar opportunity, your boxer will quickly understand that it must stay down on four legs when you or your guests arrive and that it can rejoice this way just as well.

Barking for No Reason

With boxers, barking is rarer than jumping in greeting. It is useful if the dog announces someone's arrival with a brief baying, or if it barks loudly to warn of danger. Barking ceaselessly without reason, as some dogs do from sheer boredom, becomes a nuisance, however, and it is very difficult to correct. Therefore the puppy and the young dog must learn from the beginning that barking is no way to pass the time. You can best deal with uncontrolled barking with an energetic "bad" or "no" and through diversion. When your boxer really does have a reason for barking (which may happen for the first time after it is about six months old), praise it every time.

Dogs that never bark, bay, or announce must be trained to do so: if an unauthorized stranger approaches your house, yard, or apartment, urge your boxer to bark, which is done simply by showing it how and saying "speak." It will soon become used to this and will then bay at the command.

Pulling on the Lead

A bad habit that doesn't seem so noticeably uncomfortable in the puppy as it does in the strong, adult boxer is pulling on the lead. It is a very bad habit, which must be combated consistently from the beginning. The "heel" exercise serves to do this (see page 40).

The Passion for Digging Holes

Some boxers — fortunately there are only a few — have a fatal passion: digging and burrowing in the earth. Digging incredibly fast with their front paws and snuffling excitedly, they create deep holes. Is it the scent of a field mouse or a buried bone that drives them to this quest? The habit is scarcely to be prevented with scolding or even with energetic clapping. The only course you have left is to refill the existing holes with earth and spray them with a disinfectant that has been thinned so that it won't injure the grass or plantings. This will deter some dogs from the desire to burrow, but there is no perfect remedy against this habit.

What to Do About Roaming and Fighting

Both roaming and fighting can lead to dangerous situations. Both are characteristics that are not

Training and Obedience Training

rare in the boxer, among whom roaming is particularly typical of male dogs.

Roaming dogs endanger traffic and sometimes pedestrians, too, as well as other pets and wild animals. They themselves are at risk from speeding vehicles, other dogs, and, in the country, from hunters. A well-maintained, obedient dog will never be a stray, even if roaming is its deepest desire. Boxers that tend to this behavior must therefore be particularly well supervised; unfortunately, the only sure way is keeping them on a lead. A high, thick fence does not always guarantee that a dog will remain in the yard.

For boxers with a tendency to roam, daily obedience exercises and work in the practice area as often as possible are the best "remedies." Punishment accomplishes little against this passion. Above all, never punish the dog when it returns home after a "tramping tour." On the contrary, it should be praised, for whatever it receives — punishment or praise — is the only thing it connects with its return home.

The urge to fight is, like roaming, an inborn characteristic. It can only be kept in check through training and safety precautions. With an absolutely obedient dog there are few difficulties and fights with other dogs, but if there is any question of the dog's reliability, it must always be kept on the lead in any place where it is apt to meet other dogs.

Obedience Training — The "High School" for Dogs

At the age of six months the young boxer has achieved a considerable size. It is now mature and is strong enough for the slow transition to further training.

For a boxer that is asked only to be a family dog — that is, companion and comrade — the basic obedience exercises are sufficient to ensure a good life with human beings and to avoid problems. If the boxer is to be a dependable guard and watchdog, however, or if its capabilities are to be developed purely as sport, systematic schooling is necessary.

Every Dog Needs a Task

Training places no unusual stress on your boxer, for every healthy dog needs a task appropriate to its breed. Anyone who has ever observed how impatiently most dogs at a boxer training ground await their "turn" and with what eagerness they try to or do fulfill their tasks will be convinced that the work of training is fun for them. There are exceptions, however. These are the dogs that lack the courage, the temper, the endurance, or the drive.

The goal of training is to promote abilities and characteristics that indeed are within the scope of the well-balanced temperament typical of the breed. In various trials the dogs can thus submit to proof all the talents and qualities that their character comprises.

The purpose of training and trials is the advancement of the breed.

Boxer Clubs and Associations

Prerequisite for obedience training is membership in a club or an association. The umbrella organization of dog clubs is the American Kennel Club. The oldest established breed club for the boxer is the American Boxer Club (address, see page 67). For many years it has maintained the studbook, watched over the selection of the breed (that is, determined dogs' suitability for breeding), and promoted trials and breed specialty shows. Almost everywhere a chapter is within reachable distance of your own living area. The associations permit use of the practice grounds on certain days, usually on weekends. There you are provided with advice and help, whether you are a newcomer or a practiced dog trainer.

43

Training and Obedience Training

If a boxer club or chapter is not available to you, it's usually also possible to undertake the training of your boxer with a nearby club dedicated to one of the other working dog breeds. In any case, the communication with experienced dog handlers is interesting and useful. You can find out the details of the numerous steps in schooling and trials in the special literature (see page 67). You will also learn about the trial regulations, which you can get from the boxer club or another breed association.

The Trainer

If you are determined to succeed with training your boxer, if you have time for it and much patience, you can undertake this training yourself. You can get help and direction from official helpers at dog training schools. Here the dog is not the only one that learns — the dog handler learns as well.

Another possibility is to entrust your boxer to an experienced dog trainer and guard dog helper. In this case you should be present during your boxer's training, if you can.

The Field Trial

For all working dog breeds there are many different trials. Of these the most important for the boxer are the particularly complex guard dog trials. The trial is divided into sections in which increasingly demanding tasks are set in each section: tracking, obedience, and protection. The young boxer must be at least 14 months old to compete.

The Most Important Exercises

Tracking depends on the sense of smell, the "good nose" of the dog. It must search out the scent of a track that has been laid earlier and find objects that have been laid out. This is not an exercise that is particularly appropriate to the nature of the boxer.

Training. Part of the training for a guard dog is catching a pretending culprit (a helper or a stand-in with a padded arm protector).

The most important exercises of obedience, besides those previously discussed, are stay, come here, running ahead, giving up objects, retrieving (bringing an object), and jumping over hurdles (and also retrieving while doing so). Besides this the dog must be completely uninfluenced by any sudden sound, such as the firing of a gun.

In guard dog exercises an intruder (a stand-in) must be used. This part is taken by a helper who (protected with padded clothing and leather) arouses the dog's desire to fight and to the pursuit that should greet an attack. Almost all boxers perform this task with pleasure: standing and barking, sudden attack, pursuit, and holding as a test of courage. The boxer must demonstrate its drive to fight with an unshakable grip.

Training and Obedience Training

What to Watch During Training

Every dog needs certain prerequisites, such as courage, hardiness, competitive drive, and a good constitution, to be able to grow into the demands of the training.

All commands must be brief, and hand commands must be unmistakable; the obedience of the dog is the unalterable first commandment. However, the dog must never be asked for too much.

Dog Shows

The proper term for a dog show is a breed show. this term demonstrates that a dog show is not just a beauty contest but also an event in the interest of furthering the breed. The animals are judged by the standard alone (see page 6). Thus every show provides an overview of the actual condition and level of the breed. Beside the shows of the particular breed in which only boxers take part, there are also the general and the international shows of all breeds, such as the national championship shows.

The Presentation: The dogs are presented by their owners or other handlers in a presentation ring. The conformation judge decides which dog comes closest in its external breed characteristics and in general appearance to the breed standard. The rating of the dog in competition is interesting not only for the breeder but also for every dog owner, active participant as well as onlooker.

Requirements for Participation: If you want to enter your boxer in competition, you must register it ahead of time. The deadline will be announced in dog newsletters. You will need registered pedigree papers, immunization records, and a health certificate as well as the registration fee. The dogs will be placed in different classes according to their age and, if necessary, according to their degree of training.

Character and Behavior

There is scarcely a dog that calls out so many different feelings among those who do not know it as does the boxer: enthusiasm and affection from one, fear or aversion from the other. The looks of the boxer, particularly its face, appear fierce to some; others find the appearance amusing and attractive. Anyone who knows boxers well knows that both viewpoints have grounds, for the boxer's face mirrors its whole essence in its many expressions and its nature is recognizable in its bearing and movements.

Characteristics: Inherited and Developed

The significance of character and its development rank high for boxers. From its warrior ancestors the boxer has inherited the temperament, drive, instinct, and capability to learn. These contribute to the character that enables it to be a good family dog or a dependable guard dog. Every little puppy is born with the hereditary qualities of its breed and family. The development of the individual inborn characteristics depends largely on the influences in its environment. Good characteristics can be fostered through challenge, bad ones through neglect or poor training. Thus absolute fidelity can develop from affection, but on the other hand, aggressiveness and a tendency to bite can also develop from courage and pugnacity.

Character, Temperament, and Feelings

An outstanding characteristic of the boxer is its courage, its fearlessness. It needs this pluck against the cunning of some other dogs, for the boxer itself is open and without guile. Its character may be described as honorable. It is alert, good with children, a good protector, and dependable, loyal, and ready to subordinate itself.

An unruffled, cheerful temperament is part of its character. If it is young, its spirits sparkle, and sometimes it seems as if its temperament is scarcely to be subdued. Usually from the second year on, however, it achieves the desired evenness of temper. This temperament persists even in later years. Of course its reactions are slower then, so that in age it seems quieter when its bodily activity is diminished.

The word "feelings" is little used in connection with a dog. And yet, with my boxers, I have always had the experience that they express feelings that I do not understand as drives or instinct but as emotion: The joy of my dog when I come home; the deep, lasting depression when I go away; and its sympathy if I am ever very sad.

Drive — a Stimulus for Certain Functions

All drives are inborn. Each single drive represents a force that releases a certain type of behavior. This happens involuntarily. The elementary drives of self-preservation and procreation of the species are the strongest forces. For the dog owner it is important to know these drives to be able to understand the behavior of his or her dog.

The drive for self-preservation, the drive for battle and self-defense, can be used positively in training and particularly in obedience training. The drive to hunt and bring back prey should, however, normally be suppressed; otherwise the boxer can develop into a wild animal.

Its strong drive to protect, which belongs to the social drives, guarantees security in the house and outside it.

Character and Behavior

The drive to take care of and nurture is also very pronounced in the boxer. Originally it was directed only to the dog itself and to its young. Through domestication the function has become broadened, and today the dog takes possession of all that it sees as belonging to family and home. It watches children responsibly and will, followings its care drive, if it is not prevented, lick them, just as it cleans itself or licks a wound or the way a bitch cleans her puppies with her tongue and massages them.

The drive for nourishment as a drive for self-preservation appears today only in wild animals, since most dogs are well kept and nourished.

The sex drive serves to maintain the species and, as in ancient times, rules the bitch in heat (see page 62) and the male dog as soon as he gets the scent of the female in heat. Containing this drive is scarcely possible, since it would fight against nature.

Instinct, the "Steering Apparatus"

Instinct is harder to define than drive; like drives, the instincts are also involuntary activities. They function as part of the inherited consciousness, that is, the inherited total of experiences of millions of years. Instincts do not directly release functions but steer them. Thus, for example, the hunting and baiting drive urges the dog to the pursuit of the wild animal, whereas instinct urges it to hunting behavior, tracking the animals with its sense of smell.

Instincts can also have a warning function for the dog. Very often it will be clear that the dog is conscious of dangers long before they are perceptible by their senses. If a boxer wakes up suddenly alert and continues to remain that way, its instinct is protecting it.

Intelligence — Memory Performance

Anyone who has been intensively involved with boxers is amazed again and again by the numerous evidences of their intelligence. Certainly the boxer does not possess understanding or reason in the sense that humans do, but the astonishing "intellectual" capabilities, its brain powers, are undisputed: an outstanding memory, a talent for combining and associating concepts, and an ability to learn, the capacity for rapid perception and reaction as well as a good memory. Like all abilities, these vary from individual to individual. They must first be developed and then be constantly promoted. A boxer with which nobody bothers, that is not addressed and is not developed, remains indifferent; its eyes are expressionless. The more the boxer is spoken to, the more small and large tasks that are set for it, and the more closely it is involved in the life of

Watchfulness is an important characteristic of the boxer. It is a good, fearless watchdog.

the family, the more versatility its intellectual capacities will develop. They improve slowly from year to year, and eventually the "wisdom" of an old boxer is expressed in its eyes.

Being Understood and Understanding

Beginning with the trained ways for making themselves understood, such as the request to go out, many boxers are able to share their wishes and needs with their masters. They are quite inventive in their modes of expression (see page 50). This is especially true of boxers whose intelligence and talents have been cultivated through attention. They also have an astonishing ability to understand their masters, and this does not mean only the practiced commands. If all the words, concepts, and names that a boxer understands — that is, to which it responds appropriately — were ever written down it would constitute a long list, perhaps even a small notebook.

Character Guarantees

The inner qualities of the boxer, which are innate to its breed and are defined in the standard, can only be useful to it and its environment if the dog is of guaranteed character. Qualities present should be

● an even temperament
● responsibility
● a good defense and protective drive
● fearlessness and hardiness
● loyalty to its master

This ideal combination is not present in every boxer. Weakness, anxiety, fearfulness, or bad nature, anchored in the character by inheritance, can also be part of the personality. This happens seldom, for mostly such characterics are inherited. The guarantee of character of the parents is therefore a prerequisite for breeding.

What Makes the Boxer a Good Family Dog?

Devotion, Loyalty, and Bonding to the Master
The boxer is a family dog in the true meaning of the word. Its devotion and loyalty are offered equally to every member of the family. Its behavior in response to individuals can, on the other hand, be entirely different — playing with children, alert with the person who feeds it, expectant and ready to take off with its master — but its basic attitude remains the same. Its devotion is so great that it takes hardship and deprivation on itself, if need be, will even suffer pain, not to have to be separated from its people. Loyalty is also bound in with its devotion. For no other person will it stand up so steadfastly as for its master or for the family. It appears that the boxer also expects loyalty from them, for it tends to jealousy. Therefore you should, if you can, avoid praising or admiring other dogs in its presence.

Love of Children
The boxer is especially nice with children, as it demonstrates time and again, although this quality of boxers is also frequently doubted. Boxers that are shy of children or become at all aggressive are exceptions and are almost always dogs that have had bad experience with children or have behavioral disturbances for other reasons. A great inclination toward children is embedded in the nature of the boxer, in its distinct drive for protection and nurturing and in its drive to play. A healthy boxer of guaranteed character will not permit a stranger to do anything to a child of its family.

Character and Behavior

Watcher in the House and Protector Abroad

The boxer is a good watchdog by nature. It is vigilant and has sharp senses and a sure instinct. Because it matures relatively late, however, you can only begin to count dependably on its watchfulness after one-and-a-half to two years. Some boxers need some "assistance" at first to develop into good watchdogs (see page 43). Most show early through growling and barking, however, that they are masters of their duty of warning and watching. In the course of doing so they make fine distinctions in their tonal expressions, whose meaning the boxer owner can decipher with some success (see Sound Utterances, page 50).

A watchful boxer guarantees that no one with bad intentions can come near your house or apartment unnoticed. Added to this is the frightening effect of its powerful appearance and grim face when it barks angrily. It is known that in a serious situation, friendly and playful boxers can, to the surprise of their owners, grab hold of an intruder and refuse to let go.

The company of a boxer on lonely walks and hikes offers a great security. It must of course be obedient, of reliable character, and also, of course, grown up. A young dog is not a reliable protector, and there is no relying on a shy or a cowardly boxer. It is useful only to scare off attackers by its appearance.

Breed-Typical Behavior

Sense Perception

Drive and instinct determine the way the dog behaves, and the sensory organs provide the connection to its environment. General knowledge of the sensory organs will therefore make the particular ways boxers behave understandable to you.

In play the puppy also seeks the warmth and nearness of the mother.

The sense of smell: The highly sensitive olfactory sense of the dog, which is tied to the well-developed sense of taste, brings about the major portion of its perceptions. In contrast to human beings, it depends upon its nose rather than on its eyes, which explains its efforts to smell and sniff everything. Even the short, twitching movements of the end of its nose and the expansion of the nostrils are signs of intensive perception with the olfactory sense. The boxer's smell sensitivities are considerably stronger than those of humans because the smelling surfaces in the interior of its nose are increased significantly by numerous folds.

The sense of sight: In comparison with various other dog breeds the eyes of the boxer are relatively large. Because of their forward placement, however, the boxer's visual field — even if greater than that of humans — is narrower than that of, for example, the collie, the Doberman pinscher, and many other dogs, whose eyes are situated at the sides of their heads. For the boxer, which assesses its surroundings visually with alertness and interest, turning its head and "taking a look around" are therefore typical. Dogs are farsighted. Since they see more in one plane than three-dimensionally, their sense of smell or of hearing helps them to the exact confirmation of their perception.

Character and Behavior

The sense of hearing: Dogs have an especially good sense of hearing. Their range goes far beyond the hearing range of humans. They can perceive soft sounds over long distances, as well as high tones that are not audible to the human ear (see the "soundless" dog whistle, page 39). This explains why dogs will suddenly growl, bark, or cock their ears, if there is apparently nothing to see and nothing to hear.

The sense of touch: This is not markedly different from that of human beings. The endings of the sensory nerves, which are distributed over the body of the dog, perceive different stimuli, above all that of touch. Some places are particularly sensitive: the end of the nose, tongue, the lips, and the balls of the feet. In addition, the lips are furnished with long whiskers (these should never be cut).

Sound Utterances

"Talking aloud" is actually the proper description for the sound utterances, and with the boxer it really does seem as if it has its own language. The ability for this varies with the individual boxer. Furthermore, a boxer that is frequently addressed can express itself differently from one to which only a little attention is paid. If you spend time with your boxer you will soon understand its "language."

Pain is expressed in a very high tone — squealing, howling, also whimpering.

Joy can also be expressed in high tones, which are also mixed with a darker tone like a "song."

"Hunting fever" is expressed with a high, short bell tone, if for example the boxer barks at a cat that has fled up a tree or — which ought not to happen — it is pursuing a wild animal.

The boxer barks at other dogs in different tones.

A friendly greeting is expressed through a deep, uniform barking.

Enmity and lust for battle are signaled by a challenging, sharp bark with increasing volume.

A deep, angry growl is the forewarning. Even the growling, however, has different shadings with which the boxer expresses its feelings.

Great comfort is expressed by some boxers as a rumbling similar to muttering.

Puppies have their own speech. The first sounds are a fine peeping — little announcing notes for the mother. Later the high-toned attempts to bark signal a bold desire to explore and already something of the fearless nature of the boxer.

Characteristic Movements — Body Language

In special measure the boxer has the desire and the capability for sharing its feelings. The spoken language alone is not sufficient for this; body movements and miming belong to "self-expression."

Its joy is expressed, as for all dogs, through wagging the tail, whereby it waves its little cropped tail strongly back and forth or even lets it circle. When it is very happy it wags its whole hind end and a kind of serpent wriggle results. If it feels comfortable and free, its gait can also be very elastic, almost like a hunting cat.

A feeling of being at ease shows in the position that it adopts: lying on the side, the legs stretched before it, or on the stomach, the head close between the front feet with glances in the direction of its master. If it feels very happy and content, it rolls on its back, remaining in this position, head on one side, and waits for someone to scratch it. This position shows its feeling absolute security.

A sign of pleasure and exuberance is rolling, in summer in damp grass or in winter in snow.

If it is sad it curls up tightly.

If it feels "insulted" it turns away and refuses to be talked to.

Anxiety and uncertainty are signaled by tucked-under tail; this goes to guilt, as well, in which it also sinks its head a bit and slows its steps as it approaches.

Offering a paw is mostly a learned gesture, but some boxers do make this gesture of begging or affection on their own. Even in puppies the lifting of the paw is observed as playful groping, and many adult dogs touch lovingly in play, but also inquiringly, with the paw extended toward their playmate, whether human or animal.

Movements in sleep: The quivers and running movements of a dog in sleep, often accompanied by small sounds, show us that it dreams.

Miming — Mirror of Feelings

The gaiety of nature that makes the boxer so beloved can be seen in the variety of its facial expressions.

His expressive eyes can look questioning — with head held at an angle — beseeching, even devoted, but the look can also be roguish, challenging, angry, or mean.

The play of the ears accompanies the facial expression. In a boxer with cropped ears it is especially expressive: alert, interested, suspenseful, or expectant if it holds the ears upright or points them. If it turns them sideways — some can even do this in different directions — it shows that it is curious but also mistrustful. Laying the ears back means watch out, be alert. If at the same time the fur on the neck and back begins to bristle, this is a sign that it wants a fight and is eager to attack. A boxer whose ears have not been cropped can have this range of meaningful expression to a very small degree only.

Its facial expression: The boxer does not show its teeth, but when it fights, its face, with its highly drawn upper lip and wide-open mouth, takes on a fearsome expression. The opposite is its facial expression when it draws back its lips, which looks as if it is going to laugh.

Meeting People

"Welcoming ceremonies": The boxer loves to express its love and affection stormily, and if you do not tell it to control this, you can be knocked down, scratched, or lovingly licked. Many pieces of clothing are ripped or shopping bags torn out of the hand by boxers that are not well brought up, who jump and are allowed to give their joy free rein (see page 24). The well-trained boxer expresses its joy at reunion in another way: the little tail wags strongly, it wiggles with its whole body, and dances in a tight little circle; it lets out a joyful bark or "sings" in every possible tone. Only slowly does it calm down. A dog biscuit distracts it.

Trusting strangers: If a boxer greets a stranger with friendliness, it does not mean at all that he would not be a good watchdog. The dog feels instinctively who warrants its trust (as the section Watcher in the House explains, see page 49). Boxers love to have company. This positive impulse must, however, be tactfully held within limits, so that its good ability to differentiate is not lost. Strangers should therefore probably not be permitted to stroke the dog.

If the boxer doesn't like someone: There are people whom the boxer always barks at, even when there don't seem to be any grounds for this. It simply doesn't like them. Most belong to those — as has been observed with all breeds of dogs — like the letter carrier, although he or she takes nothing away, rather brings something. It's best if your boxer is kept on the lead in such a case or sent to its bed.

Boxers and Other Pets

"Sole ruler" in the house is the status that makes most boxers feel happiest. They don't like to share the love and attention of their caretaker with other animals. But there are also many examples of friendship between boxers and various other pets.

Cats and boxers sometimes get along very well. Nevertheless, most boxers are bitter enemies of cats. These fleet animals, armed with sharp claws that can inflict dangerous wounds on the boxer, usually manage to flee successfully. If the cat fails to flee, the boxer grabs it in its jaws and shakes it briefly and jerkily; this means death for the cat. If possible, try to get your boxer used to cats as a puppy. This will save you excitement and anger.

Rabbits, hares, and hamsters or other pets and boxers can always coexist if the boxer is acquainted with the animal as a puppy and grows up with it. Nevertheless, if it is a situation in which an animal has already lived there longer or the puppy does not accept it on some ground, there will certainly be difficulties sooner or later.

Meeting Other Dogs

How a meeting between two unknown dogs will turn out is difficult to predict, even if the one dog is obedient and reliable. The majority of encounters proceed amicably. Healthy, properly maintained dogs react to other dogs according to their nature. That is, they sniff briefly nose to nose, then each sniffs the other's rear end; male dogs then lift their leg, so that their opposite number can get the scent of the urine, the "scent mark." Then nothing more stands in the way of a friendly jaunt together or a common game.

Hostility between male and female or between puppies and adult dogs is very rare. The only cause of a possible altercation then might be a behaviorally disturbed dog, one that, for example, has never had contact with other dogs or is allowed to meet other dogs only on a lead. A dog on a lead feels — properly — insecure. If necessary it would not be able to fight, so its anxiety and aggression are aroused.

The meeting between two males or two females can easily lead to strife, whether it is to establish the ranking order or out of rivalry. For this reason many dog owners when walking their dogs call out, even from a distance, to find out what sex another dog is. Then the dogs can be placed on the lead if necessary.

Caution: Do not depend on the frequently heard call "Leave your dog free — my dog won't do anything." Often the brief growl of one dog

Submissive behavior. In a battle for dominance the weaker boxer gives up by lying on its back and presenting its throat to the dominant opponent. The victor then stops fighting.

serves to open the hostilities in a split second. Any intervention is then dangerous; distraction is the best way to separate the fighters.

The Order of Dominance: The establishment of dominant ranking is a behavior pattern that the dog has inherited from its ancestors. It was a life necessity to them as pack-hunting animals. For domestic animals the establishment of dominance is merely a ritual to determine which is the strongest. Before it comes to a real test of strength the order of dominance can be established by impressive behavior alone, that is, by threatening bearing and raised fur. Sometimes it will be decided by a fight, in which the weaker will finally lie on its back and with this submissive gesture recognize its opponent as the stronger. The victor will then immediately stop fighting.

Bringing up puppies: Polly, the author's dog, with her puppies Assi and Arco. The care and supervision of the puppies occupies the bitch the whole day.

Character and Behavior

Marking and Sniffing: The male dog's wish on a walk not to omit a tree, post, or pole for sniffing and lifting his leg demonstrates the instinct to mark his territory. With his scent mark he leaves behind his "visiting card" and at the same time covers the marking of other dogs. For all males who move in the same territory this serves as a kind of communication system. Females void themselves by raising their rear ends once or twice. They are also interested in the various different scent marks, however, especially before and during heat. Since dogs perceive all their impressions most strongly through their olfactory sense, for them sniffing is the most interesting occupation in the course of their day.

The Love of Water

Again and again I have noticed that boxers love the water. They can swim well with circular movement of the front paws. They spring spiritedly after a stick that has been thrown into a pond or lake for them. Nevertheless they should not remain in the water too long or chill or exhaustion will result. The sea with foaming breakers also impels boxers to play. They like to wade in a brook or lie flat in a puddle — mostly not to the pleasure of their masters.
Caution: Great care is urged where there are currents, high waves, or steep banks.

A boxer male and two females. Left: The female boxer Isa von Hechtwasser. Jumping — to catch a ball, for example — is one of boxers' favorite games. Top right: Ever alert, the boxer observes the passing scene on the other side of the fence. Bottom: A brindled boxer female, the 1½-year-old Aggi von Grünwalder Forst in an alertly tense posture.

Uncommon Behavior Manifestations

Heavy Saliva Flow

Sweets and begged "crumbs from the table" are a factor in the development of drooling. There are also other reasons for this uncommon manifestation, however. Stress, excitement, or play with another dog can cause threads of saliva, bubbles, or foam to develop on the lips.

Eating Refuse and Rolling in Filth

Unfortunately, if the dog is allowed to run free, it will eventually find some kind of refuse and eat it. The stimulus for this behavior can be a particular deficiency in its diet. Usually it occurs in combination with rolling in filth or excrement, a need that goes back to an inherited behavior pattern. A consultation with the veterinarian about a possible dietary deficiency can be helpful.

Behavior Disorders

The Anxiety Biter

Fearfulness and cowardice lead to behavior disturbances. These are character deficiencies that can be inborn but usually are mostly developed by the wrong care and training. Both characteristics are preliminary steps in the development of the so-called anxiety biter. At the least occasion the dog feels itself driven into a corner and bites out of anxiety.

Aggressiveness

The overpowering desire to attack is also only rarely an inherited characteristic. Responsible but badly trained dogs can be aggressive. Cunning and maliciousness usually belong in the portrait of the aggressive dog. Great caution is suggested with these animals. They should not be kept in a family with children.

Causes and Possibility of Improvement

Conditions that are caused by inherited flaws can scarcely be corrected. If brain damage has been caused by illness, there is no improvement to hope for. If a dog's neurotic behavior arises from a lack of firm direction, however, proper understanding may lead to erasing the disorder. Dogs that have become cowards, fighters, and anxiety biters because they have been beaten or locked up have fewer chances to be healed of their spiritual damage. Sometimes special dog training schools can bring about improvements in "problem dogs" (addresses can be found in dog periodicals). At the first sign of a behavioral disturbance, the maintenance program should be checked immediately to see if it is appropriate for the breed and the nature of the dog.

Health Maintenance and Sickness

Dog Anatomy in Brief

The boxer has a rectangular body structure with strong bones and powerfully developed musculature.

Head: broad upper head, shortened upper jaw, undershot lower jaw (that is, longer than upper jaw and a little turned upward). The teeth number 42: 20 to the upper jaw, 22 to the lower jaw. (The teeth should not be seen when the lips are closed.)

Forequarters: This is the front half of the body, including neck, shoulder, chest, and front limbs; it supports the body. The topmost bone is the shoulder blade; it must stand in the proper angle to the forearm to ensure an elastic gait and capacity for work. The legs are sturdy and straight.

Hindquarters: This is the back half of the body, including loins, croup, and rear legs. The croup is composed of the pelvic bones, which articulate with the backbone; it is slightly sloped. The hindquarters give the main impetus during motion.

Rump: Straight, short back with powerful musculature and well-marked withers (the highest place on the back); the deep rib cage with well-arched ribs gives space for heart and lungs.

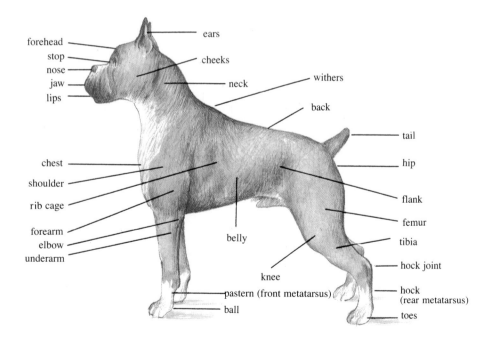

Body parts and body divisions of the boxer. It can be useful, especially for discussions with the veterinarian, to know the terms for the individual body parts and body divisions.

Health Maintenance and Sickness

Prevention of Sickness

You can do much on your own for the comfort and maintenance of the health of your boxer.

Strengthening of Natural Defenses

Your boxer needs: Measured amounts of food, with the quantities of vitamins, trace elements, and calcium appropriate to its duties and the season; much movement in fresh air, daily exercises.

Your boxer should not: become pampered; be overfed, be kept in overheated, damp, or especially cold rooms; become overstressed.

Inoculations

The important preventive measure against viruses and bacteria is the inoculation.

Initial immunization of puppies: Seventh to ninth week first injections against distemper, hepatitis, leptospirosis, and parvovirus. Three to four weeks later second shots against the above-named illnesses.

Booster shots: Yearly with combination immunization against distemper, hepatitis, leptospirosis, and rabies.

Other immunizations: Yearly against parvovirus and kennel cough.

The inoculants are harmless, and inoculated dogs pose no dangers to humans. The inoculations are entered in the immunization record; you should note the important immunizations in your dog diary.

Combating Parasites

Parasites can have a devastating effect on the comfort and health of the dog. They must be dealth with persistently. You can get the appropriate medications from the veterinarian or in a pet store.

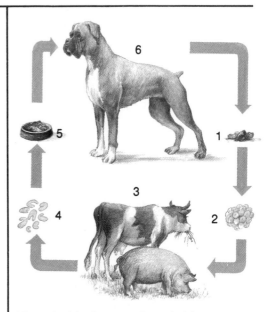

The cycle of development and spread of dog tapeworm. Eggs secreted by the dog (1 and 2) are ingested with food by an intermediate host (3) and develop into larvae in the lungs, heart, or liver (4). When fed raw organ meats (5), the boxer ingests the larvae, which develop into tapeworms in its stomach and intestinal tract (6).

External Parasites: Fleas, mites, lice, and ticks can be treated with special preparations (for example, in baths). Be careful to follow the directions on the label of the particular remedy exactly.

The annoying, bloodsucking tick, which bores its head into the skin of the dog, must be dabbed just before removal with some oil or alcohol. Then press deeply with a pair of tweezers or forceps, turn the tick counterclockwise, and carefully draw it out. There is a small electronic device for ticks and fleas that can be fastened to the collar. A wave of current, which the dog does not perceive, keeps off the parasites.

Health Maintenance and Sickness

Internal Parasites: Roundworms, which often cause diarrhea and vomiting, are 2.7 to 5.85 inches (7–15 cm) long, whitish, and appear often in puppies. The most common tapeworm is white, looks like a grain of rice [a segment can be up to 0.6 inches (1.5 cm) long] and can be seen in the feces. Whipworms are localized in the appendix and cause intermittent diarrhea; hookworms may cause severe anemia.

Symptoms of Worm Infestation: Even healthy-looking animals can be infested with worms. A very severe attack can lead to a distended belly, vomiting, and diarrhea. The surest way to diagnosis is the examination of a fecal sample by the veterinarian, who will also prescribe the appropriate medication.

Watching for Symptoms of Illness

In dogs there are various different signs of disturbed health that are easy to recognize: refusal to eat; vomiting; diarrhea; fever; weight loss; tearing eyes and discharge from the ears; warm, dry nose; swelling; pale interiors of the lips; rough, dull fur; heavy shedding (except during the season for shedding); unusual need for sleep; stiffness; dragging the rear end ("sleigh riding"); head shaking; frequent scratching (especially at the ears); and convulsions.

Each of these signs does not necessarily signal the beginning of illness. A passing, entirely harmless phenomenon might be involved. It is very difficult for the dog owner who has not had long experience in keeping dogs to make the distinction. The best thing is therefore to get the advice of a veterinarian at the appearance of any suspicious symptom.

What to Do in Case of Illness

To be able to render first aid at any time, a small dog first-aid kit should be prepared. It should contain bandaging material, cotton and adhesive tape, a disinfectant, petroleum jelly, and the medications recommended by the veterinarian; in addition, a rectal thermometer, bandage scissors, tweezers, and a snakebite kit.

First Aid for Wounds and Poisoned Wounds

The dog will heal small wounds itself by licking. For larger wounds a temporary bandage should be applied with gentle pressure; the bandage should be briefly loosened every 20 minutes. In any case the veterinarian should be called.

Poisoning

This presents itself in different forms, depending on the nature of the poison ingested. If you have any suspicion that your boxer has gotten any poisoned material while walking or in the house, you must call the veterinarian immediately and ask for first-aid measures. In the case of poisoning the help of a veterinarian is absolutely essential!

Taking the Temperature

The temperature of a healthy boxer is around 101.3 to 102.2°F (38.5-39.0°C); in young dogs it is somewhat higher. For temperature measurement the thermometer must be lubricated with oil or petroleum jelly, then carefully inserted in the anus and held there for 3 minutes; during this a helper should hold the dog securely and calm it.

Administration of Medications

Pills, tablets, or capsules go down best if they are rolled in a little ball of hamburger, or open the dog's jaws and shove the medication as far back as possible with two fingers and hold the jaws shut until the dog has swallowed.

Medications in the form of fluids or powders can, if they haven't a strong smell, be mixed with the food. Pouring them into the jaws must be done by holding the lip up at the side while the head is held up (best done with a plastic dropper). Suppositories are lubricated with petroleum jelly and shoved in as deeply as possible; a rubber glove is worn for this.

The Most Common Ailments

Digestive Disturbances
Vomiting and diarrhea that occur in isolated instances are not cause for alarm, especially not with puppies and young dogs (they are mostly food dependent). If the symptoms persist, however, the cause may be worms, poisoning, or other illness. The veterinarian must be consulted.
Constipation occurs frequently in dogs and is mostly the result of wrong diet or feeding with bones. Some raw beef liver, milk, or a piece of butter can act as a laxative.
For a slight stomach disorder the dog will help itself by eating grass that it then vomits.

Respiratory Illness
Coughing, rattling breath sounds, and eventually the onset of fever indicate an illness that demands immediate veterinary intervention.
   A dry cough, even without fever, is the first sign of adenoviral cough (also called kennel cough). It especially attacks puppies. Recently an inoculation against it has been developed.

Tumors

Unfortunately the boxer has a tendency to growths and abscesses; old dogs are especially affected by them. Tumors can appear on any body surface, interior as well as exterior. Treatment by the veterinarian is necessary.

Hip Joint Dysplasia (HD)

Hip joint dysplasia is a pathological change of the hip joint, which affects the dog by interfering with movement and making standing difficult. It can lead to painful joint inflammation and to permanent disability. The predisposition to this illness is inherited.

Severe Infections

The sicknesses on the following list can be inhibited by regular inoculations. Affected animals must be treated by the veterinarian.
Distemper is nearly incurable in young dogs. It is signaled by listlessness, fever, vomiting, and connective tissue inflammation and later also by convulsions and paralysis.
Hepatitis is a contagious liver infection. High fever, diarrhea, inflammation of the upper respiratory passages, and occasionally jaundice of the eye are the characteristic symptoms.
Leptospirosis is hard to recognize. Diarrhea, vomiting, and a foul smell from the jaws can indicate the illness.
Parvovirus illness is a dangerous infectious illness only recently recognized, which is mostly fatal to puppies. It presents as stomach and intestinal disturbances with bloody diarrhea.
Rabies, which can be transmitted to humans by the saliva of an infected animal, has increased in recent years. In many countries inoculation of dogs is mandatory. Immunization is urgently suggested for every dog. The disease is incurable. It attacks the nerves and the brain. Biting frenzy, fury, severe convulsions, paralysis, and difficulty swallowing are some of the manifestations of the illness.

Health Maintenance and Sickness

Age and the End

The boxer, whose health is susceptible in youth but then stabilizes itself, tends toward illness again from the seventh year of life on. His life expectancy is not high, but nevertheless it varies greatly. It is not unusual for a boxer to live only 7 or 8 years; 13 to 14 years, on the other hand, is considered an astonishing age for this breed.

The first signs of beginning age can appear in the sixth year. These are white hairs on the jaw, a "white beard," which makes the healthy, lively boxer seem older than it is. Nevertheless it can retain its strong appearance and the tone of its body for a very long time. A prerequisite is the right kind of care, which also preserves its urge to be active and its high capacity for work.

Age: Eventually the time comes when its playfulness wanes, its gait grows slower, and it spends more and more time in its basket. In this period of its fading life the bond between it and its master or the family is especially close and the ties more fervent. It now needs much attention but even more rest and, if illnesses strike it, the treatment and care that will relieve its pain.

Parting: If the dog is incurably ill, if it is suffering and shows no more pleasure in life, the time of parting has come. It should then, after discussion with the veterinarian, be let go. The decision is a hard one for every dog owner, but it would be selfish if we were to prolong the pain and suffering of the dog. Putting the dog to sleep is free of pain — a narcotic is overdosed. Do not leave your four-legged friend, which has accompanied you always, alone at this moment. Hold it in your arms, so that it feels secure as it falls asleep.

Breeding and Raising Puppies

Requirements for Breeding

Many owners of boxer bitches want the dog to have young at least once in her life. This is understandable, especially when people assume that the experience of birth and the raising of puppies will mature her and that such characteristics as devotion and alertness will be deepened. This has not, however, been proven. It should be understood, moreover, that "wanting puppies" is somewhat different from breeding.

Heat

About every six months, mostly in spring and in fall, the bitch will come into heat (estrus). This period lasts for three weeks, during which the dog behaves restlessly to an increasing degree and discharges some blood. It is important that you establish the first day of the blood discharge and note it, since you can then calculate the day of fertility. In the first phase of estrus, pre-estrus, the bitch attracts males to be sure, but it is not yet time for mating. Only when the bloody discharge diminishes and becomes somewhat glassy-colored does the phase of estrus begin in which the bitch will accept a male. This usually occurs only on day 13 but could begin on day 7.

The first period of heat appears in the young bitch anywhere from seven to nine months. She must not under any circumstances be bred at this time but only after the third period of heat; she is then fully grown and developed. During the whole period of estrus she should remain under supervision so that she cannot be mated against your wishes, and she must be especially well looked after.

The Sire and the Mating

Long before the time of mating a sire can be chosen, so that mature consideration of all factors of the inheritance is possible and comparisons can be made. In this the counsel of an experienced breeder is a great help.

At the time of mating the dog and the bitch play together for a shorter or a longer time, depending on their temperament and sympathy. If it then comes to the act of mating, which is not always the case, both dogs remain bound together for ten to twenty minutes more. This natural occurrence should not be interrupted, for a forceful separation can result in injuries.

Pregnancy

Pregnancy or False Pregnancy?
Whether the bitch has conceived cannot be established with certainty at first. The behavior and the external appearance of a pregnant dog differ very little from that of one with a false pregnancy. The imaginary pregnancy occurs mostly with dogs that have not before whelped. In the fourth week after estrus the dugs of the falsely pregnant female will swell, milk may even appear, and the bitch may be a wet nurse

A mock battle. Top: The brindled boxer offers a challenge to play fight, to which the older fawn-colored boxer reacts cautiously. Center: The fawn-colored dog shows the younger dog its neck in play (submissive gesture). Bottom: Here the younger boxer submits.

for a superfluous puppy of a litter or for an orphan. If this is not possible, the bitch must be moved a great deal and diverted and receive less food. Cold compresses will reduce the swelling of the dugs. During the false pregnancy the bitch is restless and finds little objects, which she nurtures like puppies.

Care and Feeding of the Pregnant Dog

The gestation period lasts about 63 days. In this period little should change in the maintenance of the pregnant bitch, but she should be especially well cared for. However, it would be wrong to overfeed her. Instead her nourishment should be increased in value; that is, she needs more vitamins and calcium. Exercise in fresh air is good for her, but she shouldn't strain, and during the second half of the pregnancy, especially, she shouldn't jump and rush around. She will become quieter toward the end of the pregnancy. By then her body has become fuller and the dugs larger.

Preparations for the Birth

Females that are giving birth for the first time must become accustomed to the birth box early on.

It should be large enough so that the bitch has enough room to stretch out completely. Besides there must be enough room left over for the puppies, for the box will represent their "only home" for about three weeks. A size of 39 × 47

In the "nursery." Top: Six puppies may be left to a breeding bitch to bring up. Bottom: The bitch takes care of cleaning the puppies herself for three weeks.

The birthing box must be roomy, disinfected, and kept clean; it should have a changeable filler.

inches (100 × 120 cm) is sufficient. The box must also have an edge 12 to 23 inches (30-60 cm) high, so that the puppies cannot fall out in the first few days. The floor of the birthing box can be strewn with straw or newspaper strips. It is comfortable for the bitch and puppies if a cloth or unfluffy cover is spread over it; it must be changed one to two times daily for hygienic reasons.

About 14 days before the birth the veterinarian must be notified so that he or she can help right away if complications occur during the birth. The bitch will be wormed 10 days before the birth, which should prevent an attack of mawworms in the puppies. Finally, two days before the birth, the birthing box and its surroundings should be disinfected.

The Birth Process — the Litter

By her unrest and refusal of food the bitch announces the birth several hours ahead of time. The room in which the birthing box is placed should have a temperature of about 68 to 73°F

(20-23°C). Handkerchiefs and bandage material must be at hand for the emergency as well as for use as a scale. A signal of the beginning of the birth is the sinking of the body temperature and powerful panting, which can go on for hours. The bitch needs quiet. Normally it will not be necessary to interfere in the birth process. The puppies come into the world in an amniotic sac, which the bitch bites open, in order to busily lick the newborn dry. The little mewing creature scrambles right away to one of the nipples and begins to drink. An hour may pass until the birth of the next puppy, so that with a litter of nine puppies, which is not unusual, more than 10 hours altogether may pass. If before or during the birth a complication arises, the veterinarian must be called immediately.

Bitch and Puppies During the First Three Weeks

A healthy female looks after her puppies for three weeks all by herself. She nourishes and cleans them, and she keeps the box clean. She regulates the digestion of each puppy by massaging the little belly with her tongue. She also takes up the excretions. She thus becomes very stressed. In the interests of her health it is therefore firmly established in the breeding regulations that not more than six puppies should be left to her. Besides the strengthening foods with vitamin and calcium additives, the bitch can be given milk, cottage cheese, and honey.

The puppies are blind until the tenth day; they can only hear after twelve days. Nevertheless their sense of smell leads them to the source of nourishment, where the strongest wins the best place for itself. They grow from day to day, become strong, move more confidently, and after three weeks leave the "nest" ever more frequently.

In case of need, gentle stroking substitutes for the mother's massaging to excite digestion.

Development of the Puppies

The puppies now begin to explore their environment. From about the fourth week they should receive additional food, milk with some oatmeal gruel, grated beef or prepared puppy food, and additional calcium and vitamin tablets. The lively little fellows measure their strength in little battles. They react to the human with joy, in which they rush to him or her with flying ears and attempt their first barking sounds. The more freely they can move, the more objects they touch, smell, investigate, the more extensive is their development. They are in the imprinting phase. All impressions and social contacts during this period determine their later behavior. The bitch urges them with educational neck shaking or gentle pokes with the forelegs toward their bed when they are overtired. It is also very important, however, that you spend time with them: play with them, talk, and train them to be housebroken.

After eight weeks comes the time when you must give the puppies to their new owner, to whom you should also be available for advice in the future.

Useful Literature and Addresses

The Dog Care Manual by David Alderton
(Barron's)

First Aid for Dogs by Fredric L. Frye (Barron's)

The New Dog Handbook by Hans - J. Ullmann
(Barron's)

American Kennel Club (AKC)
51 Madison Avenue
New York, N.Y. 10010

American Boarding Kennels Association
4575 Galley Road # 400-A
Colorado Springs, CO 80915

American Boxer Club, Inc.*
% Mrs. Lorraine C. Meyer
807 Fairview Boulevard
Rockford, IL 61107

*As an address is almost invariably the home of an officer of the breed club, it is understandable that it can change as new
elections are held. It is wise to check with the AKC for an update on a club's address.

Index

Index

Index

Perfect for Pet Owners!

"Clear, concise…written in simple, nontechnical language."

—*Booklist*

AFRICAN GRAY PARROTS Wolter (3773-1)
AMAZON PARROTS Lantermann (4035-X)
BANTAMS Fritzsche (3687-5)
BEAGLES Vriends-Parent (3829-0)
BEEKEEPING Melzer (4089-9)
BOXERS Kraupa-Tuskany (4036-8)
CANARIES Frisch (2614-4)
CATS Fritzsche (2421-4)
CHINCHILLAS Röder-Thiede (4037-6)
CHOW-CHOWS Atkinson (3952-1)
COCKATIELS Wolter (2889-9)
COCKATOOS (4159-3)
CONURES Vriends (4880-6)
DACHSHUNDS Fiedelmeier (2888-0)
DALMATIANS Ditto (4605-6)
DOBERMAN PINSCHERS Gudas (2999-2)
DOGS Wegler (4822-9)
DWARF RABBITS Wegler (1352-2)
FEEDING AND SHELTERING
   BACKYARD BIRDS Vriends (4252-2)
FEEDING AND SHELTERING
   EUROPEAN BIRDS von Frisch (2858-9)
FERRETS Morton (2976-3)
GERBILS Gudas (3725-1)
GERMAN SHEPHERDS Antesberger (2982-8)
GOLDEN RETRIEVERS Sucher (3793-6)
GOLDFISH Ostrow (2975-5)
GUINEA PIGS Bielfeld (2629-2)
HAMSTERS Fritzsche (2422-2)
IRISH SETTERS Stahlkuppe (4663-3)
LABRADOR RETRIEVERS Kern (3792-8)
LHASA APSOS Wehrman (3950-5)
LIZARDS IN THE TERRARIUM Jes (3925-4)

LONGHAIRED CATS Müller (2803-1)
LONG-TAILED PARAKEETS Wolter (1351-4)
LOVEBIRDS Vriends (3726-X)
MACAWS Sweeney (4768-0)
MICE Bielfeld (2921-6)
MINIATURE PIGS Storer (1356-5)
MUTTS Frye (4126-7)
MYNAHS von Frisch (3688-3)
NONVENOMOUS SNAKES Trutnau (5632-9)
PARAKEETS Wolter (2423-0)
PARROTS Wolter (4823-7)
PERSIAN CATS Müller (4405-3)
PIGEONS Vriends (4044-9)
POMERANIANS Stahlkuppe (4670-6)
PONIES Kraupa-Tuskany (2856-2)
POODLES Ullmann & Ullmann (2812-0)
RABBITS Fritzsche (2615-2)
RATS Himsel (4535-1)
SCHNAUZERS Frye (3949-1)
SHAR-PEI Ditto (4834-2)
SHEEP Müller (4091-0)
SHETLAND SHEEPDOGS Sucher (4264-6)
SIAMESE CATS Collier (4764-8)
SIBERIAN HUSKIES Kern (4265-4)
SNAKES Griehl (2813-9)
SPANIELS Ullmann & Ullmann (2424-9)
TROPICAL FISH Stadelmann (4700-1)
TURTLES Wilke (4702-8)
WATER PLANTS IN THE
   AQUARIUM Scheurmann (3926-2)
YORKSHIRE TERRIERS Kriechbaumer & Grünn
   (4406-1)
ZEBRA FINCHES Martin (3497-X)

Paperback, 6½ x 7⅞ with over 50 illustrations (20-plus color photos)   Barron's ISBN prefix: 0-8120

Barron's Educational Series, Inc. • P.O. Box 8040, 250 Wireless Blvd., Hauppauge, NY 11788
Call toll-free: 1-800-645-3476 • In Canada: Georgetown Book Warehouse
34 Armstrong Ave., Georgetown, Ont. L7G 4R9 • Call toll-free: 1-800-247-7160